SEEKING JESUS
IN THE
OLD TESTAMENT

SEEKING JESUS IN THE OLD TESTAMENT

Dr. Renu Rita Silvano, O.C.V., S.T.D.

Our Sunday Visitor Publishing Division
Our Sunday Visitor, Inc.
Huntington, IN 46750

Imprimatur:
✠ Ivan Cardinal Dias
Archbishop of Bombay
August 10, 2004

The *imprimatur* is a declaration that a work is free from doctrinal or moral error. It is not implied that the person who has granted the *imprimatur* agrees with the contents, opinions, or statements expressed.

The Scripture citations contained in this work are taken from the *Catholic Edition of the Revised Standard Version of the Bible* (RSV), copyright © 1965 and 1966 by the Division of Christian Education of the National Council of the Churches of Christ in the United States of America. Used by permission. All rights reserved.

Every reasonable effort has been made to determine copyright holders of excerpted materials and to secure permissions as needed. If any copyrighted materials have been inadvertently used in this work without proper credit being given in one form or another, please notify Our Sunday Visitor in writing so that future printings of this work may be corrected accordingly.

Our Sunday Visitor Publishing Division
Our Sunday Visitor, Inc.
200 Noll Plaza
Huntington, IN 46750

ISBN-13: 978-1-59276-199-9
ISBN-10: 1-59276-199-2 (Inventory No. T250)
LCCN: 2006921707

Cover design by Troy Lefevra
Interior design by Sherri L. Hoffman

PRINTED IN THE UNITED STATES OF AMERICA

Thou hast said,

"Seek ye my face."

My heart says to thee,

"Thy face, Lord, do I seek."

(Ps 27:8)

CONTENTS

FOREWORD

"What does this text mean for me?" is the most vital question for the reader of any biblical text. "What does it mean for me?" is also the central question that stands behind the lines of this book by Renu Rita Silvano. Taking as her point of departure the fact that many biblical texts can be difficult to understand, the author sets for herself the task of commenting on passages of the Old Testament in order to offer assistance for the reading of these texts. Her primary objective is to ensure that Holy Scripture in its entirety can become a life-giving Word of God, that the reader "will go to the Sacred Scriptures and discover the face of Jesus shining through its pages" (as she says in the Introduction).

This objective is not new; the question as to how far the Old Testament can also be the "Holy Scripture" of Christians has intrigued Christian theologians from the beginning. The result of their wrestling with this issue is well known: an interpretation of the Old Testament in the light of the Christ event created the conditions for the incorporation of virtually the entire text of the Jewish Bible into that of Christians.

An important interpretive criterion of the biblical exegesis of the first Christian centuries (Patristic exegesis) was that of "usefulness." Behind this stood the conviction that the Bible in its entirety was written "for us" and that it must "make sense" (cf. Origen, *Peri-Arch* 4, 1, 7; *Hom 1K* 5,2; *HomNum* 27, 1). A principle of Patristic exegesis — above all with respect to difficult passages — was that of the interpretation of the Scriptures through the Scriptures (cf.

Origen, *HomGen* 2, 6). This principle is, however, already practiced in the New Testament itself (e.g., in passages where Paul interprets the Old Testament Christologically).

It is this very principle that this book employs. It is a Christocentric, contemplative reading of Old Testament texts, a reading of selected passages *in the light of the Christ event* and rooted in the personal faith-experience of the author. Old Testament texts are commented on with the help of texts from the New Testament. It could be objected that this work contains hardly a trace of the historical-critical method. It is true that an integral biblical exegesis can hardly dispense with this and other hermeneutical methods today. In particular, it cannot afford to disregard the historical dimension of the Bible as a collection of faith witnesses of different generations of believers, as an example *par excellence* of faith as a historical-dialogical process, of revelation as Word of God in human language. This book does not, however, set for itself the goal of being a comprehensive exegetical clarification of the biblical texts, as the author herself emphasizes in the Introduction: "Without being a scholarly and exhaustive treatise on the Old Testament . . . care has been taken to use Catholic principles of biblical interpretation." The Christological reading of the texts and the basic effort to enable the letter of the Bible to become Word of God are precisely among these Catholic principles of interpretation. The author takes these principles as her guide.

The central question of this book, "What does this mean for me," has two addressees: the author herself and the reader. Renu Rita Silvano answers this question in a very personal way; what she has to offer the reader is then not so much a scholastic-exegetical stimulus but rather an inspiration rooted in her own faith experience for the reader's personal response to the question, "And what does this text say to me?" In this sense, the book is a meaningful tool for a personal, pastoral reading of the Bible.

We owe a debt of gratitude to the author for this work. I share her hope that when it is read, *Seeking Jesus in the Old Testament* will help create a thirst for the Word of God, and that it will provide useful incentives for each reader's own dialogue with the biblical text.

ALEXANDER M. SCHWEITZER
General Secretary of the Catholic Biblical Federation
Stuttgart, Germany
August 6, 2004 (Feast of the Transfiguration)

The worldwide Catholic Biblical Federation is currently headed by Most Rev. Vincenzo Paglia, Bishop of Terni. Appointed by the Pope, he is assisted by an Executive Committee of six members (three bishops, two priests, and one woman), and the staff of its General Office in Stuttgart. Started after the Second Vatican Council by the Pontifical Council for Christian Unity, the Federation's task is to promote the pastoral biblical apostolate according to the orientations given by *Dei Verbum*.

INTRODUCTION

Jesus said, "Seek, and you will find" (Mt 7:7). This book is a small effort to seek the face of Jesus through the Old Testament books of Moses (The Pentateuch), the Psalms, and the Prophets (specifically the "later" or "classical" prophets from Amos, c.786 BCE, to Zechariah, c.520 BCE).

This work intends to reveal a fresh encounter with Jesus through the reading of the Sacred Scriptures, even if some of its texts seem obscure and difficult. Without being a scholarly and exhaustive treatise on the Old Testament seen in the light of the New Testament, care has been taken to use Catholic principles of biblical interpretation.

The fountains of the living Word can never be exhausted, however much we drink from them. This work is simply my seeking and finding of Jesus while reading through the whole Bible, including the Old Testament. My hope is that the reader will go to the Sacred Scriptures and discover the face of Jesus shining through its pages. To read the Bible page by page and walk the journey of the People of God from the very beginning, discovering the face of Jesus all the while in the background, can bring a great joy and inspiration for the humdrum events of our own daily lives.

St. Ephraem, a fourth century Doctor of the Church, has these beautiful words of wisdom for those who approach the fountains of the living word (*Commentary on the Diateressaron*, 1.18-19):

> The thirsty man rejoices when he drinks and he is not downcast because he cannot empty the fountain. Rather let

the fountain quench your thirst than have your thirst quench the fountain. Because if your thirst is quenched and the fountain is not exhausted you can drink from it again whenever you are thirsty. Be grateful for what you have received and do not grumble about the abundance left behind. What you have received and what you have reached is your share, what remains is your heritage.

The purpose of this book is to create a thirst in the readers, to bring them to the treasure of the Word of God, and to help them discover the face of Jesus, according to the inspiration of the Holy Spirit, granted to each one. By doing this, we will give witness of our love for Jesus, enrich our faith and the faith of the whole Christian community, and practice a meaningful and authentic devotion to the word of God.

St. Jerome said: "Ignorance of Scripture is ignorance of Christ." Love of Jesus must urge us to read and keep the word of God in our lives and allow it to brighten our days and nights with its truth and saving power.

The Church teaches that the New Testament is hidden in the Old Testament, and the Old Testament is fulfilled in the New Testament (Vatican II, *Dei Verbum*, Dogmatic Constitution on Divine Revelation, n. 16). The Old Testament, too, is most precious because in it we find the promises that God made about the Messiah and all the prophecies that pointed to the coming Savior. The Old Testament is very relevant for the Christians of today — through it we obtain much of Jesus' background and history.

Keeping this truth in mind, let us journey deeper into the mysterious, yet fascinating, forest of the Word of God, where every tree is a life-giving tree "with healing in its leaves." There we will find dense forests and dry patches of open ground, all kinds of colorful flowers and fruit, rivers and streams, animals and birds . . . a beautiful and refreshing landscape, and more!

The word of God will not be exhausted or run dry, for "the word of the Lord abides for ever" (1 Pet 1:25).

SEEKING JESUS...

In the Books of Moses
(The Pentateuch)

The Book of Genesis

GENESIS 1

And God said, "Let there be light"; and there was light (Gen 1:3).

The first words that we hear God speak in the Bible are, "Let there be light," and then "God separated the light from the darkness. God called the light Day, and the darkness he called Night" (Gen 1:4-5).

From my own life's experience and from that of other people I know, I have come to see that God's priority is always to dispel darkness (symbolic of all that is negative) and bring forth brightness, purity, and radiance. Without light we would all languish and become sick and die, both in body and in spirit. In the physical realm, we need the rays of the sun for our bodies and spirits. In the spiritual realm, the true light is Jesus, the Sun of Righteousness, about whom God testifies through the words of the prophet Malachi: "For you who fear my name the sun of righteousness shall rise, with healing in its wings" (Mal 4:2).

Jesus himself bears testimony to this truth when he says of himself: "I am the light of the world; he who follows me will not walk in darkness, but will have the light of life" (Jn 8:12).

St. John in turn bears witness to Jesus saying, "In him was life, and the life was the light of men. The light shines in the darkness, and the darkness has not overcome it" (Jn 1:4-5).

As a consequence, an absolutely essential element in a Christian's life is personal commitment to the Light. St. Paul teaches that God "has delivered us from the dominion of darkness and transferred us to the kingdom of his beloved Son" (Col 1:13).

Hence, "it is full time now for you [this means us] to wake from sleep . . . the night is far gone, the day is at hand. Let us then cast off the works of darkness and put on the armor of light; let us conduct ourselves becomingly as in the day" (Rom 13:11-13).

While we live in this world, we must increase our hearing ability to hear God's words: "Let there be light!" And having heard them in the various circumstances of our lives, our first priority must be to allow its creative effect to change us, to usher in order, peace, and inner joy, and then to radiate it to others.

The eye is a powerful organ in our physical bodies. While giving us the joy of sight, our eyes are also a symbol of our inner light or darkness. Jesus says to us, "The eye is the lamp of the body. So, if your eye is sound, your whole body will be full of light; but if your eye is not sound, your whole body will be full of darkness. If then the light in you is darkness, how great is the darkness!" (Mt 6:22-23). The physical and the spiritual are linked.

Jesus is the Light of the world. He is the Light that dispels darkness from the very beginning of Creation. He will remain forever the Light of life. The book of Revelation shows us the ultimate image of the City of God: "And the city has no need of sun or moon to shine upon it, for the glory of God is its light, and its lamp is the Lamb. By its light shall the nations walk" (Rev 21:23-24).

GENESIS 2 and 3

I will put enmity between you and the woman, and between your seed and her seed; he shall bruise your head, and you shall bruise his heel (Gen 3:15).

The man called his wife's name Eve, because she was the mother of all living (Gen 3:20).

He placed the cherubim, and a flaming sword which turned every way, to guard the way to the tree of life (Gen 3:24).

These texts can point to Jesus. He is the seed of the woman, he becomes the tree of life, and the bride's desire is for him, the King.

Jesus and His Mother

It was the Son (seed) of the Virgin Mary of Nazareth who, in fact, bruised or crushed the head of the serpent by his paschal mystery of death and resurrection. (The last enemy that Jesus destroyed was death — see 1 Cor 15:26).

Jesus addressed Mary as "woman." At the very beginning of his public ministry and the manifestation of his glory, Jesus said to his mother at Cana, "O woman, what have you to do with me? My hour has not yet come" (Jn 2:4).

Jesus called her "woman" again when his hour had come and he was hanging on the cross: "When Jesus saw his mother, and the disciple whom he loved standing near, he said to his mother, 'Woman, behold, your son!' Then he said to the disciple, 'Behold, your mother!'" (Jn 19:26-27).

The hour of Jesus, the new Adam, is closely linked with the hour of Mary, the new Eve, the mother of all the living. When the hour of Jesus came (see Jn 13:1), when Jesus was glorified on the cross, he gave his mother her definitive mission, that of becoming the mother of all his disciples, that is, of all the living, of all those who believe in him. Thus, we are her children and she is our mother.

On the other hand, when the serpent tempted Eve she looked at the tree and its fruits for her own pleasure (see Gen 3:6), and accepted the half-truth told her by the serpent, "You will not die . . . you will be like God, knowing good and evil" (Gen 3:4-5). Unlike the second woman, Mary, the first woman, Eve, looked only to her own personal benefit.

The Good News tells us about the angel of the Lord bringing God's message to Mary (Lk 1:26-38). All his words about the child to be conceived in her womb are for the good of all humankind, and not just for Mary's personal benefit. She has found favor with God to bring into the world his Son who will save the world. So, the angel told her, "you shall call his name, Jesus" (Lk 1:31). And Mary gave her consent in faith not just for herself but for the salvation of all humanity.

Jesus is the *seed*. He is the grain of wheat that dies and bears much fruit. Jesus said, "The hour has come for the Son of man to be glorified. Truly, truly, I say to you, unless a grain of wheat falls into the earth and dies, it remains alone; but if it dies, it bears much fruit" (Jn 12:23-24).

We learn from the last book of the Bible, the book of Revelation, that Jesus, the seed, having fallen into the ground and died, is now for us the tree of life. We see the beautiful river of life flowing and "on either side of the river, the tree of life with its twelve kinds of fruit, yielding its fruit each month; and the leaves of the tree were for the healing of the nations" (Rev 22:2). There is also Jesus' earlier allusion, "To him who conquers I will grant to eat of the tree of life, which is in the paradise of God" (Rev 2:7).

Disciples too, who believe in him, are called to follow his example and, like seed, to die in order to produce much good fruit, expressed in the love of neighbor.

"To the woman, God said, 'Your desire shall be for your husband, and he shall rule over you'" (Gen 3:16b). This text has usually been understood as words of reproach and physical punishment for Eve, because she had listened to the serpent's voice. But as I meditated on these words I thought of the reality of my own experience of the rule of my Beloved in my life, namely, the Lordship of Jesus in my life. It dawned on me that these words of God did not just refer to the bodily dimension of a person (in this case, of a woman). Rather, they touched upon the spiritual dimension of each believer, who is a member of the Body of Christ and who in turn is the spouse of Christ.

Indeed, for every Christian who professes that Jesus is Lord, listening *in the Spirit* to these words of Genesis can be a liberating experience. Let me explain: my favorite way to address Jesus is "My Lord and my King!" Yes, I desire him at every moment of my life. "My soul thirsts for thee... as in a dry and weary land where no water is" (Ps 63:1). I am a consecrated virgin who longs for Jesus the Beloved, and for his rule in my life. Only he can fulfill me. I keep repeating many times during the day, "Lord, your kingdom come, your will be done in my life." There is nothing more for me to desire than his words and his instructions. "More to be desired are they than gold... sweeter also than honey and drippings of the honeycomb" (Ps 19:10).

It was not always like this. There was a time in my life when I sought my own pleasures in a quite foolish and self-centered way. But in his loving kindness, Jesus met me one day and breathed his Spirit into me in a new way. He made me taste the sweetness of his love and the goodness of his words. He continued to form my mind, my will, my speech over the years, till now I can say that there is a mutuality between us, my desire is for him and his desire is for me. "I am my beloved's, and his desire is for me" (Song 7:10). Jesus has led me out of darkness into his wonderful light. Hence, his rule in my life is my desire, and my desire for him helps me overcome obstacles to my spiritual growth and fruitfulness.

While I know that I am still not perfect, "I am not ashamed, for I know whom I have believed, and I am sure that he is able to guard until that Day what has been entrusted to me" (2 Tim 1:12).

The rule of Jesus does not oppress or violate my rights, as the rule of people in this world does. In fact, because he rules me I can be free and know that I am protected from all that is harmful for me. Behold, his rule or lordship has made me bloom.

The Church is the bride of Christ. Each of us is a member of the Church, the body of Christ. Together, as a community of the faithful, we constitute the bride of Christ. The Holy Spirit is the animating force, the spark that kindles our desire for Jesus. For "no one can say 'Jesus is Lord' except by the Holy Spirit" (1 Cor 12:3b).

The perfect example of the beloved who was totally open to the rule of God in her life, and whose sole desire was for God and his will, is Mary the mother of Jesus and our mother. She is the New Eve. May she accompany us every step of our lives, sharing with us her great desire for Jesus and for the full coming of his kingdom. Then all will fall in line in our pilgrimage of faith, hope, and love here on earth!

GENESIS 6:1-6

When men began to multiply on the face of the ground, and daughters were born to them, the sons of God saw that the daughters of men were fair; and they took to wife such of them as they chose (Gen 6:1-2).

The LORD saw that the wickedness of man was great in the earth, and . . . the LORD was sorry that he had made man on the earth, and it grieved him to his heart (Gen 6:5-6).

In this passage, the sacred writer narrates a mysterious story about marriages between "sons of God" and "daughters of men." In other words, between heavenly beings and human beings. The passage is liable to be misunderstood if taken literally, as some interesting movies on the subject have in fact done. However, for a correct interpretation, we must try to understand the intention of the sacred author regarding why this strange passage was put into the book of Genesis.

In the times when this passage was written, the mythological histories of many pagan nations claimed such relations between their ancestors and the gods. These people practiced fertility cults, had temple prostitutes, et cetera. It is my opinion that the sacred writer wants to point to this as yet one more in the succession of several events of sin (which began with the sin of Adam and Eve) — indeed as a final step in the development of sin. For in this story is seen the human beings' stark refusal of who they actually are: human beings, creatures, the work of God's hands.

The desire to be divine themselves (that is, in no way subordinate to God) has caused a rupture in the relationship between creatures and their Creator, and in turn as well among human beings themselves. We can see this in chapter three of Genesis when, going against God's command, Adam and Eve ate of the fruit of the tree of the knowledge of good and evil, and immediately were filled with guilt, fear, and shame. When questioned about it by God, they began to blame one another. Far from accepting their weakness together, and far from standing in their hitherto solidarity with each other (in which God had created them), they showed themselves now in fact in alienation from God and each other. Such was the consequence of their wanting to be gods themselves!

But now, let us turn our gaze to look at Jesus. In contrast to this longing of human beings to become divine and their refusal to acknowledge their creatureliness, Jesus shows himself to be totally different. Jesus was and is and will always be the only-begotten divine Son of God (Heb 13:8). He is the Word of God who was with God from the beginning; indeed, he was God from the beginning (Jn 1:1). Yet, Jesus

> *did not count equality with God a thing to be grasped, but emptied himself, taking the form of a servant, being born in the likeness of men. And being found in human form he humbled himself and became* obedient ... *(Phil 2:6-8, emphasis added).*

By accepting to be a servant (someone obedient), Jesus reversed all the evil that human beings had brought into the world by their pride and disobedience. He thus revealed the love of God very concretely, the love that existed in God's heart for his creatures, you and me, from the beginning of creation. Jesus neutralized the evil effects of sin by his perfect obedience to God's will and his humility. Thus he reconciled us to God and to one another:

> *God shows his love for us in that while we were yet sinners Christ died for us ... we also rejoice in God through our Lord Jesus Christ, through whom we have now received our reconciliation (Rom 5:8, 11).*

God's will is for us too to conquer and become victorious and reign gloriously with Jesus. The secret of our fulfilling this will is our readiness and determination to accept our creaturely condition and to behave in truly human ways.

St. John Chrysostom, in his homily on St. Matthew's Gospel, confirms,

> As long as we continue to behave as sheep, we are victorious. Even if ten thousand wolves surround us, we conquer and are victorious. But the moment we become wolves, we are conquered, for we lose the help of the shepherd. He is the shepherd of sheep, not of wolves . . . Jesus says, "My way makes you more glorious and proclaims my power . . . My grace is sufficient for you, for my power is made perfect in weakness. This is the way I made you."

If still, in this Third Millennium, we find that we human beings, in spite of being disciples of Jesus, have not stopped grasping for infinite power and glory, or are still constantly discovering within ourselves the desire for an exalted position in the eyes of the world, or we still somehow believe that we are indeed gods and that "lesser" human beings should bow down before us and always let us have our own way, then perhaps it could be that we have stopped truly and urgently seeking the face of Jesus.

Let us seek his face again as we re-read the words of Paul's letter to the Philippians (Phil 2:6-11). And let all our approval and delight in life come from Him who is the Lord and in whom we too reign, "provided we suffer with him in order that we may also be glorified with him" (Rom 8:17). The real question then is not about gods inter-marrying with human beings, but about human beings wanting and allowing themselves to be transformed into "sons and daughters" of God (cf. Rom 8:15-17).

GENESIS 14

When Abram had defeated those who had taken his kinsman Lot captive, he brought him back,

And Melchizedek king of Salem brought out bread and wine; he was priest of God Most High. And he blessed him ... And Abram gave him a tenth of everything (Gen 14:18-20).

Melchizedek is called both a king and a priest of the Most High God (even before the Levitical priesthood could be established). He offers Abraham a meal of bread and wine. He pronounces a blessing over Abraham and he receives tithes from Abraham in exchange for his protection. Abraham, "our father in faith," bows respectfully before Melchizedek, receives his blessing, and offers tribute.

Melchizedek is recognized as a type of the Messiah. Psalm 110:4 declares, "The LORD has sworn and will not change his mind, 'You are a priest for ever after the order of Melchizedek.'"

Seeking the face of Jesus in this text, we see that in fact it was Jesus, the Messiah, who fulfilled the eternal priesthood (it was only foreshadowed in Melchizedek). This is explained and described beautifully in the letter to the Hebrews, chapter seven. Jesus, the High Priest, exercises his perfect priesthood, which is not derived from the priesthood of Aaron, who was of the tribe of Levi, since Jesus is of the tribe of Judah, and the Son of David. Jesus received a royal priesthood by virtue of being the Davidic messiah, and is thus compared to Melchizedek.

The name, the titles, the character of Melchizedek all foreshadow the characteristics of Jesus. He appears with "neither beginning of days nor end of life" (Heb 7:3); thus he foreshadows Christ, the eternal priest. His name Melchizedek means: my king is justice or righteousness; king of Salem means: king of peace. Jesus is the king of justice, righteousness, and peace. It is Jesus who brings justice and peace to the world. Also, the solemn oath of Psalm 110:4 does not apply to the Levitical priests, who are sinners and mortal, and who pass on their priesthood from one generation to the next. The oath is addressed to the King-Priest, to the true Son of David, who is Jesus. He is innocent and immortal, and he brings a new and everlasting covenant, signified by the bread and wine of the Eucharist.

It follows that the face of Jesus, appearing between the lines of Genesis 14, is the radiant face of a king of peace, the just one who comes to bring justice to the nations and peace to the whole world. This Priest offers gifts on our behalf and pronounces blessings upon all who come to him for protection and salvation.

GENESIS 22:1-19

This chapter gives us the tender picture of a father with his beloved and only son. However, here the picture is not of holding and cherishing the son. Rather, Abraham, the father, is preparing to give up his son for his first love; that is, for God. And the son walks alongside his father carrying the wood for the burnt offering.

How can we not at once see the face of Jesus in the background here and recall the sacrifice that God the Father made of his only and most beloved son, Jesus Christ, for the sake of the world and for each one of us. And Jesus, too, one with the Father and in obedience to him, voluntarily laid down his life to redeem us. "God so loved the world that he gave his only Son" (Jn 3:16).

There is a particularly touching moment when Abraham's heart is seemingly broken even more. On the way, he hears his wood-laden son call out, "My father!" (Gen 22:7). On hearing these words, there must have been a storm of feelings whipped up within Abraham that threatened to sweep away all his resoluteness. Yet, with unwavering faith he was able to reply tenderly, "Here am I, my son" (Gen 22:7). Isaac said, "Behold, the fire and the wood; but where is the lamb for a burnt offering?" (Gen 22:7). And Abraham, with a tortured heart, found himself replying, "God will provide himself the lamb for a burnt offering, my son" (Gen 22:8).

Isaac, too, foreshadows Jesus. Just as the young Isaac carried the wood of the burnt offering on his shoulders, the Messiah later carried his cross on his own shoulders, and was, in fact, crucified on it. Nailed to and hanging on the cross, Jesus cried out, "Father," so many times. Even before the crucifixion, while praying in the garden of Gethsemane, Jesus thrice cried out, "Father, let this cup pass from me . . ." (Lk 22:42). From the cross Jesus cried out, "Father, forgive them . . ." (Lk 23:34), and "Father, into your hands I commit my spirit!"(Luke 23:46). And surely the Father's heart must have been wrung too. Yet he did not waver from his saving love for *all* his children, that is, for us. He let his beloved Son die on the cross for us, and for our salvation, "to gather together the scattered children of God" (Jn 11:52).

Abraham's answer to Isaac about what God would do had both a literal and a deeper sense: *God* would provide the lamb. And God provided the lamb to take the place of Isaac, as well as the Lamb of God, God's own Son, Jesus Christ, to take the place of all of humanity. For, God "did not spare his own Son but gave him up for us all" (Rom 8:32).

Abraham is the figure of total faith and generosity toward God, and his faith was reckoned to him as righteousness. But the righteousness of God goes beyond all imagination; his merciful and generous love are infinitely abundant. Whereas Abraham's son did not die, God's eternal Son *died*, rose again, and now lives forever as Savior and Lord of the whole of humanity!

The face of Jesus can be seen here both in the person of Isaac and in the ram that God provided for the burnt offering. A new factor here is that Jesus personally and voluntarily offered his sacrifice of himself,

> *For this reason the Father loves me, because I lay down my life, that I may take it again. No one takes it from me, but I lay it down, and I have power to take it up again (Jn 10:17-18).*

GENESIS 37-50

The story of Joseph, son of Jacob (Israel), has the sketch of the face of Jesus clearly imprinted in it. Joseph is the beloved son of his old father, so his brothers are jealous of him. They cannot accept his prophetic charism of the word of knowledge, nor his innocence and humor. One day they sell him to strangers. They tell lies to their father about his fate. Joseph is sold and ends up in Egypt, and in this foreign land becomes an instrument of God's wisdom and knowledge to all, especially to people in authority, all the way up to the Pharaoh. Nevertheless, Joseph has to face many trials and difficulties. He is sexually tempted and put into prison for his integrity. In prison he helps people who benefit by his word of knowledge or prophecy, but they forget him once they have been helped by him.

However, God's anointed cannot be hidden forever. Eventually, Pharaoh sets Joseph up as a wise, efficient, and trustworthy administrator over all his land and people. During a great famine which affects the entire area, when Joseph's brothers, who had cruelly sold him into slavery years earlier, come to buy grain (from a long-lost brother whom they no longer recognize), they have to bow down before him as to a lord, just as Joseph had prophesied to them in their youth!

Eventually Joseph brings it about that his father and brothers and whole family should come to live in comfort and honor in Egypt. But when Jacob dies, the brothers are suddenly again afraid of Joseph, lest now he pay them back for all the evil they have done to him. But Joseph is magnanimous to them, "Fear not, for am I in place of God? As for you, *you* meant evil against me; but *God* meant it for good. . ." (Gen 50:19-20, emphasis aded).

Is not the face of Jesus clearly seen in this story? Jesus, the beloved Son of the Father, greatly endowed with all the gifts of the Spirit, who worked wonders and preached the word of God to his people, was hated by his own, just as Joseph was. St. John says, "He came to his own, and his own received him not" (Jn 1:11). In fact, they were jealous of him when they heard his words of wisdom and saw the marvels that he worked, that is, when he gave signs of what the Scriptures had foretold about the Messiah. The priests, scribes, and Pharisees, all of them were jealous of him and hated him and wanted to do away with him. What was even more serious was that one of his closest friends, one of the Twelve, Judas Iscariot, actually sold him for a small sum of money to the chief priests and scribes.

And yet Jesus did not hold the sins of any of them against them. He forgave them. Joseph said to his brothers, "You meant evil against me, but God meant it for good." Jesus too, when the people had nailed him on the cross, wanting to kill him and get rid of him forever, forgave them saying, "Father, forgive them; for they know not what they do" (Lk 23:34).

It is also clear that God had a good purpose in all this, which was fulfilled. "Christ has been raised from the dead... For as by a man (Adam) came death, by a man (Jesus) has come also the resurrection of the dead. For as in Adam all die, so also in Christ shall all be made alive... Death is swallowed up in victory" (1 Cor 15:20-22, 54).

Those of us who are fortunate enough to believe in Jesus and to obey the Good News can also live with him each day in his glory, even though we may have to go through many trials and hurts. The mystery of the Communion of Saints convinces us that death is not the end, resurrection will follow:

"O death, where is thy victory? O death, where is thy sting?"... Thanks be to God, who gives us the victory through our Lord Jesus Christ (1 Cor 15:55, 57).

The Book of Exodus

EXODUS 2-4, 33-34

And the people of Israel groaned under their bondage, and cried out for help, and their cry under bondage came up to God. And God heard their groaning, and God remembered his covenant with Abraham... And God saw the people of Israel, and God knew their condition... God called to him out of the bush, "Moses, Moses!" And he said, "Here am I"... Then the LORD said, "I have seen the affliction of my people and have heard their cry... I know their sufferings, and I have come down to deliver them... Come, I will send you to Pharaoh that you may bring forth my people, the sons of Israel, out of Egypt" (Ex 2:23 – 3:10).

The word *mercy* is not found in this account. Nevertheless the whole story of the liberation of the Jews from Egypt is a tremendous story of divine mercy. It is also the foundation of the Jewish/Christian belief that God intervenes in human history. God is a personal God who cares for the well-being of his creatures. In his mercy, God stays close to his people. He feels with them. He does not remain aloof or hidden.

Here, God chooses his servant Moses — at first, a very reluctant Moses — to be the agent of deliverance for his people. One can feel the intensity of the compassion and faithfulness of God, the loving Father. The sacred writer uses very human images here to show how God heard, listened to, and knew the condition of the Jewish slaves in Egypt and responded to their cry.

Even when his people sinned against him, God's mercy was ready to bring them back again provided they did not harden their hearts to his grace. It has always been God's stated will to save the sinner: "The LORD passed before Moses, and proclaimed, 'The LORD, the LORD, a God merciful and gracious, slow to anger, and abounding in steadfast love and faithfulness...'" (Ex 34:6ff).

In this Exodus event, it is easy to see how Jesus is prefigured. The same mercy of God is highlighted as we continue to read the events of the history of the people of God, and it reaches its climax when God sends *another* Moses (one far greater than the Moses of the Exodus story), that is, his own Son Jesus, into the world. Aware once again of the great urgency of intervening, God heard the groaning of millions of men and women who were under bondage to sin and evil. The people needed a deliverer. And God sent Jesus to deliver us from bondage and sin and bring us to the land flowing with salvation and loving relationships. "God shows his love for us in that while we were yet sinners, Christ died for us" (Rom 5:8).

> But when the time had fully come, God sent forth his Son, born of a woman, born under the law, to redeem those who were under the law, so that we might receive adoption as sons. And because you are sons, God has sent the Spirit of his Son into our hearts, crying, "Abba! Father!" (Gal 4:4-6).

St. John emphasizes the truth that "the only Son, who is in the bosom of the Father, he has made him known" (Jn 1:18). This making the Father known to human beings through the Jesus event reveals God in the most profound mystery of his being. He is always surrounded by *unapproachable light* (1 Tim 6:16); yet, through the revelation of Jesus, we now can know God above all in his mercy and loving relationship with us (Tit 3:4).

Pope John Paul II explains well how Jesus makes the compassion of God visible to us:

> It is precisely here that "his invisible nature" becomes in a special way "visible," incomparably more visible than through all the other "things that have been made": it becomes visible in Christ and through Christ, through his actions and his words, and finally through his death on the Cross and his Resurrection. In this way, in Christ and through Christ, God also becomes especially visible in his mercy . . . Not only does he speak of it and explain it . . . but above all he himself makes it incarnate and personifies it. He himself, in a certain sense, is mercy. To the person who sees it in him and finds it in him God becomes "visible" in a particular way as the Father "who is rich in mercy" (Eph 2:4).
>
> The truth revealed in Christ, about God the "Father of mercies" (2 Cor 1:3) enables us to "see" him as particularly close to man, especially when man is suffering, when he is under threat at the very heart of his existence and dignity (Pope John Paul II, Encyclical Letter *Dives in Misericordia*, On the Mercy of God, n. 2, pp. 7-9).

This God of mercy is the one whom we meet right from the beginning of creation till the end of the world, but especially in the book of Exodus. God calls out to Moses and sends him to bring deliverance to his people. Unlike Moses, who made so many objections and excuses against the vocation being given him, Jesus willingly took up the task and emptied himself of all the glory that was his. He became a human person in order to redeem humanity (Phil 2:6-11). "When Christ came into the world, he said, '. . . Lo, I have come to do your will, O God'" (Heb 10:5-7). At the right time, the incarnate Jesus became the expression of the Father's compassion and saving love for his people.

The Exodus story led to the Mosaic Covenant. It contained the Ten Commandments, which expressed the new way to be God's people. It stressed *right relationships*. So too, the new Moses, Jesus, in a New Covenant of right relationships, stressed that we human beings too must "be merciful, even as your (heavenly) Father is merciful" (Lk 6:36). This has become an essential condition for entrance into the kingdom of heaven (Mt 5:7).

Jesus declared that one day we will be judged according to the mercy we have shown to others. He went so far as to say that all acts of mercy done to others were actually, if unknowingly, done to *him*, to his very person (Mt 25:31-46).

Hence, each one of us is called to love and have compassion in our hearts for everyone, especially for a neighbor in need, because the love of God is found only in those who show mercy (1 Jn 3:17). And we are most like Jesus when we show mercy and compassion, just as the Father shows mercy and compassion without reserve.

EXODUS 25:17-22

Then you shall make a mercy seat of pure gold . . . There I will meet with you, and from above the mercy seat, from between the two cherubim that are upon the ark of the testimony, I will speak with you of all that I will give you in commandment for the people of Israel.

God promised Moses that he would meet with and speak to his people from the "mercy seat." The mercy seat was a seat built above the ark in which the tablets of the covenant were placed. The Lord would reveal his glory seated on the mercy seat, and speak his words to his people.

I am touched greatly by the name of the place from where God promises to reveal his glory and his words to his people, namely, *the mercy seat*. This leaves me with no doubt at all that God's great characteristic is Mercy. So many people today have a notion of God as a very harsh and stern Deity, who is far away above the skies, a God who does not really heed the cries of the suffering and the poor. But nothing can be further from the truth! Our God is a God of mercy and compassion; in fact, God's mercy makes him keep on crying out to us:

Hear, O my people, while I admonish you; . . . if you would but listen to me . . . O that my people would listen to me . . . (Ps 81:8, 11, 13).

One concrete way in which we can listen to the voice of the Lord today is by trying to behave like him in our relationships with others. Jesus too tells his disciples, "Be merciful, even as your Father is merciful" (Lk 6:36). These words echo and develop what Exodus contains. The only way to experience the mercy of God is to show mercy to others, especially to those most in need of mercy. Here is one example from Exodus:

If ever you take your neighbor's garment (cloak) in pledge (pawn), you shall restore it before the sun goes down; for it may be your neighbor's only clothing to use as a cover; in what else shall that person sleep? And (God says) if he (the neighbor) cries out to me, I will hear, for I am compassionate (Ex 22:26-27).

Jesus brings God's mercy closest to us. Through him we receive the confidence of approaching the "mercy seat." The author of the letter to the Hebrews emphasizes this fact, saying:

Since, then, we have a great high priest who has passed through the heavens, Jesus, the Son of God, . . . Let us therefore approach the throne of grace with boldness, so that we may receive mercy and find grace to help in time of need (Heb 4:14, 16).

Indeed, let us approach the God of mercy and compassion with confidence, because in and through Jesus Christ our Lord, we are children and co-heirs of the Kingdom of God, provided we do whatever he tells us, and love our neighbor as ourselves.

EXODUS 26:1 – 31:18; 34:1 – 40:33

These sections of the book of Exodus give us details about the instructions that God gave Moses when he was with God twice on the mountain forty days and forty nights (Ex 24:18; 34:28). The instructions had to do with the building of the tent of meeting with an ark and mercy seat, anointing of priests, liturgy and liturgical requirements, keeping of the Sabbath, et cetera.

God tells Moses that his sincere wish is to dwell with his people. His word/testimony ("written with the finger of God" on the tables of stone, Ex 31:18) is to be kept inside the ark that is to be built in a certain way, and the mercy seat is to be built upon it with two cherubim on either side. It is in the tabernacle that the word will be kept and from the mercy seat the Lord will speak to his people, and his glory will rest on it (Ex 26:34; 30:6). And all of these will be covered with curtains and veils.

God instructed Moses how there should be curtains of fine twined linen looped and clasped together to the tabernacle (Ex 26:1-6; 36:8-13, 35, 37). Then there should also be curtains of goats' hair, goatskins and rams' skins for a tent over the tabernacle to cover it (Ex 36:7-19). Moses is to prepare the priests' garments in a particular way, he is to anoint and ordain Aaron and his sons as priests.

Moses is to make an altar to burn incense upon, and "put it before the veil that is by the ark of the testimony, before the mercy seat . . . And Aaron shall burn fragrant incense on it . . . Aaron shall make atonement once a year; with the blood of the sin offering of atonement he shall make atonement for it once in the year throughout your generation; it is most holy to the LORD" (Ex 30:6-11).

Later on, the temple replaced the mobile tent of meeting, and the holy of holies was fixed in the very heart of it. The mercy seat held the luminous glory of God, which still remained, hidden and unapproachable.

As I read these amazing descriptions, I am reminded of what the Gospels say regarding the veil of the temple at the moment when Jesus was taking his last breath on the cross. St. Luke writes: "It was now about the sixth hour, and there was darkness over the whole land until the ninth hour, while the sun's light failed; and the curtain of the temple was torn in two" (Lk 23:44-45). St. Matthew writes, "And Jesus cried again with a loud voice and yielded up his spirit. And behold, the curtain of the temple was torn in two, from top to bottom" (Mt 27:50-51).

The sacred author of the letter to the Hebrews sees Jesus as the supreme High Priest, and says, "when Christ appeared as a high priest . . . *he entered once for all into the Holy Place*, taking not the blood of goats and calves but his own blood, thus securing an eternal redemption" (Heb 9:11-14, emphasis added).

At the moment of Jesus' last breath, the veil that hid God's presence from his people was rent asunder and the death of the Lamb of God became for us the way of reconciliation and union with the Father once and for all (Rom 5:11). God's earnest desire is for us to have access to him, and this has been made possible only through Jesus our beloved Lord and Savior.

Now we have entered the holy of holies with him, but not as tourists. He has taken us into the very presence of God so that our lives can be united to his, and we can draw close to him with our faith and good works. Jesus is our way to the Father, and we need not be in the dark any more, he has brought us the light, so that we too are to be "light" to all those groping in the darkness of sin and all kinds of evil.

So, let us all cry out to Jesus, the Lamb of God who is worthy, and who alone can take the scroll from the holy of holies and open its seals, "for you were slain and by your blood you did ransom us for God, from every tribe and tongue and people and nation, and you have made (us) a kingdom and priests to our God, and (we) shall reign on earth" (Rev 5:9-10). Worthy are you Lord Jesus Christ!

The Book of Leviticus

LEVITICUS 6

Reading through the whole book of Leviticus, one is struck by the very active, watchful, responsible, and authoritative role of the priest. Aaron and his sons were appointed to be the priests. (Aaron was the brother of Moses, their parents were from the house of Levi — Ex 2:1; 3:14). The priest offered all the ritual sacrifices and made atonement on behalf of individuals or the whole community. The individual or the people had only to accept their condition and bring their prescribed offerings to the priest and the priest did the rest of the work. Another work of the priest was to keep the fire burning all night on the altar and watch that it did not go out.

> *The fire on the altar shall be kept burning on it, it shall not go out; the priest shall burn wood on it every morning, and he shall lay the burnt offering in order upon it, and shall burn on it the fat of the peace offerings. Fire shall be kept burning upon the altar continually; it shall not go out (Lev 6:12-13).*

The people either individually or as a community brought their sin offerings and gave them to the priest to offer on the altar. The sins of the people were thus offered up as the priest offered the sin offerings on their behalf.

To relate all this to Jesus, I am reminded of the sacrament of Reconciliation where the person confesses sins with full confidence that, as God's representative, the priest's forgiveness and prayer is effective. Only today the "sin offering" is made in words by confessing one's sins; in Leviticus the confession was made in action by offering burnt offerings, sin offerings, peace offerings, etc.

Moreover, the gifts offered by the priest remind us of the Sacrifice of the Holy Eucharist wherein the priest, in the person of Jesus, offers the gifts of bread and wine to the Father, which are then transformed into the precious body and blood of Jesus, our life-giving food and drink. Leviticus 6:18 says of the burnt offerings, "whoever touches them shall become holy!" How much more holy will those become, who not only touch but eat and drink the sacred body and blood of Jesus Christ, the Son of God, provided we come with expectant faith and active love!

LEVITICUS 13-15

The priest in Leviticus functions as a doctor as well. It is his duty to make sure that every one is healthy and "clean" in the community. So he is given the task of examining persons with skin diseases, diagnosing their sickness, and pronouncing them "clean" or "unclean." Anyone whose skin eruption or disease is diagnosed as leprosy is pronounced "unclean" and made an outcast until the person is cured.

> *The leper who has the disease shall wear torn clothes and let the hair of his head hang loose, and he shall cover his upper lip and cry, "Unclean, unclean." He shall remain unclean as long as he has the disease; he is unclean; he shall dwell alone in a habitation outside the camp (Lev 13:45-46).*

This role of the priest as a kind of physician reminds me of Jesus, the eternal High Priest (cf. Heb 5:10; 6:20; 7:3; 9:11-14) who knows and sees our diseases and heals them. The Levite priest could only diagnose and pronounce "unclean," but Jesus is both Priest and Healer. He diagnoses, cleanses and heals all our diseases. We have seen this happen time and again in the Gospel accounts, and throughout the history of Christianity. We have only to open up our wounds and sicknesses with full faith and confidence before his Divine Mercy.

Let us recall the many times in the Gospel when lepers were touched and healed by Jesus. For example:

> *When Jesus had come down from the mountain, great crowds followed him; and there was a leper who came to him and knelt before him, saying, "Lord, if you choose to, you can make me clean." He stretched out his hand and touched him, saying, "I do choose to. Be made clean!" Immediately his leprosy was cleansed. Then Jesus said to him, "See that you say nothing to*

anyone; but go, show yourself to the priest, and offer the gift
that Moses commanded, as a testimony to them" (Mt 8:1-4).

In the Old Testament, a leper had to "dwell alone outside the camp," as we saw in Lev 13:46. But this New Testament leper came to Jesus and knelt before him and expressed words of faith in Jesus. And Jesus healed him. Jesus sent him to the priest who would confirm his healing and pronounce him "clean," as was pre-scribed in the book of Leviticus:

> *The LORD spoke to Moses, saying: This shall be the ritual for*
> *the leprous person at the time of his cleansing: He shall be*
> *brought to the priest; the priest ... shall make an examination.*
> *If the disease is healed ... the priest shall command that two*
> *living clean birds ... be brought for the one who is to be*
> *cleansed ... On the seventh day he shall shave ... all his*
> *hair ... wash his clothes, and bathe, and he shall be clean. On*
> *the eighth day he shall take two male lambs without blem-*
> *ish ... and the priest shall make atonement before the LORD on*
> *behalf of the one being cleansed (Lev 14:1-32).*

Although Jesus sent the lepers he healed to the priests for the ritual of cleansing, yet there is also the incident of the ten lepers who were cleansed by the word spoken by Jesus. One of them, who was a Samaritan, did not need to go to the priest. He turned to Jesus, recognizing his real Healer, and brought his sacrifice of praise and thanksgiving to him, and Jesus praised his faith and con-firmed his healing:

> *[Jesus] was passing along between Samaria and Galilee. And*
> *as he entered a village, he was met by ten lepers, who stood at*
> *a distance and lifted up their voices and said, "Jesus, Master,*
> *have mercy on us!" When he saw them, he said to them, "Go*
> *and show yourselves to the priests." And as they went they*

were cleansed. Then one of them, when he saw that he was healed, turned back, praising God with a loud voice; and he fell on his face at Jesus' feet, giving him thanks. Now he was a Samaritan. Then said Jesus, "Were not ten cleansed? Where are the nine? Was no one found to return and give praise to God except this foreigner?" And he said to him, "Rise and go your way; your faith has made you well" (Lk 17:11-19).

The Book of Numbers

NUMBERS 1:52; 2:2ff

The people of Israel shall pitch their tents by their companies, every man by his own camp and every man by his own standard... they shall encamp facing the tent of meeting on every side.

This picture of the people pitching their tents by companies, once the glory of the Lord was seen over the Tent of Meeting, brings to my mind a New Testament incident where the people sat by companies in the presence of the Lord Jesus. He fed them at length on his words and then gave them bread and fish to eat in the wilderness:

> *[Jesus] said to them, "How many loaves have you?"... they said, "Five, and two fish." Then he commanded them all to sit down by companies upon the green grass. So they sat down in groups, by hundreds and by fifties... And those who ate were about five thousand men, besides women and children (Mk 6:38-44 and Mt 14:21).*

The book of Numbers continues, "And those to encamp before the tabernacle on the east, before the tent of meeting toward the sunrise, were Moses and Aaron and his sons" (Num 3:38).

So too, as Jesus took the "five loaves and two fish he looked up to heaven, and blessed and broke the loaves, and gave them to the disciples to set before the people" (Mark 6:41), I can imagine the people sitting facing Jesus (God-with-us), with the disciples also sitting in front facing Jesus.

The evangelists tell us that those who were fed by Jesus were "five thousand men, besides women and children" (Mk 6:44 and Mt 14:21). This cultural custom of counting families according to the number of their men-folk had been handed down from the Old Testament. In the passage from Numbers we see that the companies were numbered according to the number of men. The women and children were not numbered, although they were very much present in the companies (cf. Num 1:20, 22). The total number of the companies was "six hundred and three thousand five hundred and fifty" men (Num 1:46). The Levites, too, who were to take care of the tabernacle, numbered only their men. This kind of patriarchal orientation had more to do with the culture of the times than with the essentials of religion.

In the wilderness of Sinai, God fed his people constantly upon his word. Jesus, too, fed the people on his word (Mk 6:34). Jesus also gave them nourishment for their body, just as God did in the wilderness when He gave them manna from heaven. Jesus went beyond the bread and the manna and gave himself to his people, saying, "I am the bread of life. Your fathers ate the manna in the wilderness, and they died. . . . I am the living bread which came down from heaven; if any one eats of this bread, he will live for ever" (Jn 6:48-51).

Yet another element which strikes us as we read the account of Numbers or the account of Jesus feeding the people is that there is a certain order and decorum that is observed in the presence of the Lord, whether in the wilderness of Sinai, or the wilderness of Bethsaida (Lk 9:10, 12; Mk 6:30). When the Lord is present and his presence means everything to us, when he is enthroned in his rightful place, all else falls into place. When Jesus becomes the center of our lives and attention, we will not lack for any good gift, for every need will be met by the Lord who cares for us.

NUMBERS 5:2-3

Put out of the camp every leper, and every one having a discharge, and every one that is unclean through contact with the dead; you shall put out both male and female, putting them outside the camp, that they may not defile their camp.

This text of Numbers names three kinds of people who are to be treated as outcasts because of "uncleanness." These are lepers or people with skin diseases, people with any kind of discharge, and people who had any contact with a dead body.

We have considered the lepers earlier (in the section from the book of Leviticus). In this section we will consider the other two kinds of unclean people.

Put out of the camp every ... one having a discharge ... both male and female, putting them outside the camp, that they may not defile their camp.

This practice was carried out quite strictly, and people with any kind of discharge from the body, for example, the natural monthly flow of blood during a woman's menstruation period (cf. Lev 12:2), or any other kind of discharge in both men and women, were to be out of reach of every other person and thing in the camp or house. They were just put out of the camp.

This is not a practice of those days alone, even in our days in certain cultures, we find the same beliefs about being clean/unclean, especially during a woman's menstruation period. The girl or woman is required to sit outside the house or in some corner of the house, where other members of the house cannot come near her. On such days she cannot sit and eat with others nor can she attend any liturgical celebrations. The good news is, however, that in our modern culture, more and more people, especially women, are giving up these social taboos.

I'd like to remember here that when one enters into contact with Jesus, then every thing becomes pure and clean and liberated. The very encounter with his presence brings freedom from any bondage. For example, once when Jesus was on his way to the house of Jairus, whose twelve-year-old daughter was dying,

> *A woman who had suffered from a flow of blood for twelve years and could not be healed by any one, came up behind him and touched the fringe of his garment; and immediately her flow of blood ceased. And Jesus said, "Who was it that touched me?"*
>
> *"Someone has touched me; for I perceive that power has gone forth from me." And when the woman saw that she was not hidden, she came trembling, and falling down before him declared in the presence of all the people why she had touched him, and how she had been immediately healed. And Jesus said to her, "Daughter, your faith has made you well; go in peace"* (Luke 8:43-48).

The woman knew that she was considered unclean and she was not allowed to go among people. Yet, she longed to go near Jesus, if only to touch the fringe of his garment. She believed in the holiness and power of Jesus. She knew in her spirit that he was not bound by regulations and rituals. So she had the courage to push her way into the crowd, after perhaps covering her face well so that no one would recognize her. She reached close to Jesus and stretching out, managed to touch his garment, and immediately she knew that she was healed.

Then the happy woman probably thought that she could escape and no one would know about her adventure and healing, and so she could not be punished for coming into a crowd. But Jesus knew that she had touched him "for power has gone forth from me," he said. The woman could no longer hide herself and had to share with everyone what had happened, and she received a double blessing, Jesus declared her "well," as the priest would do in the Jewish tradition when anyone was healed or made clean (cf. Lev 12:6-8). And Jesus gave her his "peace," which is a gift of wholeness, far deeper than the physical healing.

> Put out of the camp... every one that is unclean through contact with the dead... that they may not defile their camp.

In this context, a parable comes to mind that Jesus told the questioning scribe in the presence of his disciples. The scribe, a doctor of the law, asked Jesus, "And who is my neighbor?" Jesus replied by narrating the parable of the Good Samaritan who had "proved neighbor to the man who fell among the robbers."

> A man was going... he fell among robbers, who stripped him... and departed, leaving him half dead. Now by chance a priest was going down that road; and when he saw him he passed by on the other side. So likewise a Levite... passed by on the other side. But a Samaritan.... when he saw him, had compassion... and took care of him. And the next day he took out two denarii and gave them to the innkeeper, saying, "Take care of him; and whatever more you spend, I will repay you when I come back" (Lk 10:29-37).

Notice what the priest and the Levite do when they see the man lying in a pool of blood on the road. Both of them, one by one, pass by on the other side. These were religious leaders. They should have been good shepherds! The man lying on the road was most probably a Jew, for he was traveling from Jerusalem to Jericho. Yet, both the priest and the Levite ignore him and go off to their religious business. Why? Because they *slavishly* obeyed the prescription of the law:

> Whoever touches the dead body of any person shall be unclean seven days... Whoever touches a dead person, the body of any

man who has died, and does not cleanse himself, defiles the tabernacle of the LORD, and that person shall be cut off from Israel (Num 19:11-13).

The priest and the Levite did not want to take any risk of becoming "unclean" for seven days. In their rigid or narrow approach to the law, they narrowed their hearts too, and felt no compassion for the wounded man. They did not even care to come close and see whether he was only wounded or whether life was still in him. If they had done that they would not have become unclean. But their hearts were closed to others and tied up with keeping the prescriptions to prove themselves "clean."

Jesus told this parable to point out who are those who are truly fit for eternal life. This stranger acted out of love. "He had compassion." He was a Samaritan, whom the Jews did not associate with, an outcast and not a law-abiding Jew. Yet, this person truly kept the law to its perfection.

Just before Jesus told this parable the scribe had asked Jesus, "what shall I do to inherit eternal life?" and Jesus had reminded him of the well-known Jewish commandments, "love the Lord . . . and love your neighbor as yourself" (Lk 10:25-28; Deut 6:6; Lev 19:18).

For Jesus, the things that make a person unclean are not external things, rather, they are internal things. To the Pharisees, who had objected that Jesus and his disciples did not wash their hands before eating, Jesus said,

What comes out of the mouth proceeds from the heart, and this defiles a person. For out of the heart come evil thoughts, murder . . . false witness, slander. These are what defile a person; but to eat with unwashed hands does not defile a person (Mt 15:18-20).

In fact, Jesus even touched dead persons and not only did he remain clean but his touch gave life to those who had been dead.

A man came from Jairus' house and said, "Your daughter is dead; do not trouble the Teacher any more." But Jesus answered him, "Do not fear; only believe, and she shall be well." And when he came to the house, he permitted no one to enter with him, except Peter and John and James, and the father and mother of the child... And the people laughed at him, knowing that she was dead. But taking her by the hand he called, saying, "Child, arise." And her spirit returned, and she got up at once (Lk 8:49-56).

Jesus' word cleanses us from all defilement (Jn 15:3). His word is liberating and gives life. Jesus did not abolish the law, he fulfilled the law (cf Mt 5:17-20). And he calls us today to break free from our narrow mentality of just keeping the rules and regulations because we want to present a righteous facade. Jesus says, "For I tell you, unless your righteousness exceeds that of the scribes and Pharisees, you will never enter the kingdom of heaven" (Mt 5:20).

NUMBERS 6:24-26

The LORD bless you and keep you: The LORD make his face to shine upon you, and be gracious to you: The LORD lift up his countenance upon you, and give you peace.

God commanded that Aaron and his sons pray this beautiful priestly blessing upon the people. Once again, the face of Jesus appears here! As I read the words of this God-given blessing, I was immediately reminded of the special prayer that Jesus gave his disciples to pray, the "Our Father" (Mt 6:9-13, Lk 11:2-4). As I went deeper into this eternal prayer and its meaning, it struck me that the Aaronic Blessing is a beautiful complement to it, and can indeed be used as a response to the prayer that the Lord Jesus taught us. Chronologically the blessing was given first, but then God always takes the first initiative to bless us even before we learn how to pray and ask in prayer!

"The LORD" is the name that the people of God used to address their Lord God, Yahweh. Jesus addresses the Lord God as "Abba, Father," and he also taught us to call God *"Our Father!"*

"Who art in heaven." God dwells in the heavens and at the same time he dwells among us. Hence, the Lord *Abba* can make "his face shine upon us."

"The LORD bless you." The name of the Lord is holy, *"hallowed,"* and with that hallowed name we are blessed and made holy.

"Thy kingdom come, thy will be done." When the Lord makes "his face shine upon" us, when he lifts up "his countenance upon" us, his Kingdom comes amidst us and we desire for his will to be done, here and now and for ever, "on earth as in heaven." Such is the experience of any one who is in love. For such a person in love, the one desire and longing is that the beloved's presence remain forever: "Thy kingdom come." The beloved's desires become our own desires: "Thy will be done," here, now, and always.

We pray, *"Give us this day our daily bread,"* and the blessing says, "The LORD be gracious to you." What else is needed? The Lord our Abba is so gracious, we only have to ask like a child believing in his providence and generosity, and our trust will never go empty, for he is gracious and loving to all who call upon him. In his graciousness he provides for every creature, even for birds who "neither sow nor reap nor gather into barns, and yet your heavenly Father feeds them. Are you not of more value than they?" (Mt 6:26).

"Forgive us our trespasses as we forgive." "The LORD make his face to shine upon you." In times of distress and sin, it almost always seems that God has hidden his face from us and abandoned us: "For our soul is bowed down to the dust . . . Rise up, come to our help . . ." (Ps 44:25-26). When we experience forgiveness and are able to forgive others, the face of the Lord shines brightly upon us and banishes all darkness and sin till we too are filled with light and become light to others.

"Lead us not into temptation, but deliver us from evil." "The LORD keep you ... The LORD lift up his countenance upon you, and give you peace." When the Lord our Father keeps us and gives us peace, can any evil overcome us? No, for then we are strong and bright. When the Lord and I gaze upon each other's face, his countenance upon mine, then the experience is that of total well-being and wholeness. At such a time no temptation can overcome us or lead us away from the beloved.

This indeed is the gift of peace that the Father gives us. This is the peace for which the priest prayed using the words of this Blessing. And this peace and well being is our weapon with which you and I can overcome any trial, be they daily trials and temptations or end-time trials to come.

How beautifully intertwined is our prayer, our longing, and God's own response and blessing!

NUMBERS 9:15-22

On the day that the tabernacle was set up, the cloud covered the tabernacle, the tent of the testimony; and at evening it was over the tabernacle like the appearance of fire until morning . . . As long as the cloud rested over the tabernacle, the people remained in camp. Even when the cloud continued over the tabernacle many days, the people . . . did not set out. Whether it was two days, or a month, or a longer time, that the cloud continued over the tabernacle, abiding there, the people of Israel remained in camp and did not set out; but when it was taken up they set out.

Two points strike me as we read this passage: First, readiness to follow the Lord's timing with reverence; and second, the joy of encamping in God's presence.

(1) Readiness to follow the Lord's timing with reverence. Normally, when people are on a journey, they try their best to reach their destination as fast as possible. Any delay on the way, any waiting makes them impatient and upset. Isn't that true of us too? But the people of Israel moved forward and stopped at the Lord's command (Num 9:18). The Lord manifested his presence in the cloud that rested over the tabernacle in which were kept the tablets of stone of God's commandments given to Moses on Mount Sinai. The Lord's presence was seen in a cloud by day and fire by night over the tabernacle, that is, on the mercy seat (Ex 25:21-22; Lev 16:2). The people continued their journey when the cloud by day or the fire by night was lifted up.

For the people of Israel, the important thing was to follow the Lord's timing at every step. When he stopped, they stopped, when he moved, they moved. There could not be any hastiness or traveling according to their likes and dislikes. Nor could any one go on their own, for they believed that they were a community that had to stay together. Their anointed leader, Moses, made them keenly aware of the Lordship of God who cared for them and was with them as they journeyed through the wilderness.

We, who are followers of Jesus and children of God, the Father of our Lord Jesus Christ, must want to be disciples wholeheartedly. When we walk with the Lord, it is good to remind ourselves that time is his gift to us, and for him there is no limitation of time for he is eternal. In the midst of a very hectic yet fulfilling life, we may sometimes find that it is possible for us to go faster and achieve more, but we are slowed down by the limits put upon us by people in authority. Or when suddenly from a very successful life in the apostolate, we land up in a hospital bed with some sickness, such an experience may leave us very discouraged and even bitter.

But it is at such times that we can recall Jesus' presence with his disciples who were called first of all "to be with him" (Mk 3:14). When the cloud and the fire rested on the tabernacle, the people encamped and that was their time of "being with him" and listening to his loving words that strengthened their faith. They did not know how long they would have to wait or how long they would have to walk on; or even why God chose certain days to stop. Their love and faith strengthened their energies and they persevered. They believed all that God had promised them and they obeyed his will.

As I read the Scriptures, I am amazed to find how at every step, Jesus followed the will of God according to God's timing and not his own. To take just one example, remember the day in Capernaum when Jesus had spent all his time healing all kinds of sick people and lepers, including people with unclean spirits and Simon's mother-in-law. And before dawn the next morning he went away to a lonely place "and there he prayed." But the people pursued him and wanted him to come back into the village again and stay. Jesus who had just waited on his Father in prayer knew that the Father wanted him to continue his journey, and he said, "Let us go on to the next towns, that I may preach there also;

for that is why I came out" (Mk 1:35-38). Jesus did not give importance to popularity and fame, but only to the saving will of God the Father.

Sometimes Jesus' timing does not seem proper even to his disciples and friends. Recall the day when the sisters of Lazarus, Martha and Mary, sent people to inform Jesus, "Lord, he whom you love is ill." The story then continues, "Now Jesus loved Martha and her sister and Lazarus. So when he heard that he was ill, he stayed two days longer in the place where he was" (Jn 11:3-6). This sounds strange to us! Jesus, who cared much about the sick and healed them, seemed not to respond positively when news of Lazarus' illness came to him. Yet, Jesus knew what he was about.

Finally, four days after Lazarus' death, Jesus decided to go to Bethany. There both the sisters of Lazarus complained that if Jesus had come when he first got their message, Lazarus would have been alive (Jn 11:21, 32). And Jesus grieved with them: "Jesus wept" (Jn 11:35). Yet, even in times of high emotion, his focus was not diverted from the Father's saving will. Jesus knew that God wanted to manifest his glory to all by raising Lazarus from the dead. *This* would be the time of glory!

Not infrequently, *we* decide the right timing for ourselves. We decide when we want to stay, where and how long we want to stay, or why we should not stay in this or that place. Especially when we meet with a sad incident, we want to change location, so as to escape the sad memory. But, God never wants us to escape from difficult situations, rather with him we can face any challenge that comes before us. As the psalmist says, "With you I can break through any barrier, with my God I can scale any wall" (Ps 18:29).

In the wilderness of Sinai the people met with many hardships, but trusting that God is faithful to his promises, they kept going and reached the Promised Land. Sadly, when Jesus was crucified and died on the cross, even his disciples did not persevere in their faith. They forgot all that Jesus had told them about his resurrection (cf. Mk 8:31; 9:31; 10:32-34). St. Luke describes how two disciples were running away from Jerusalem, the place where Jesus had been crucified, to Emmaus. (Mark also writes about them in 16:12.) They were very sad and disappointed with what happened to Jesus. They had their own ideas and expectations of Jesus, which were not fulfilled the way they wanted. So they tried to escape from there (Lk 24:13-35). But it was not the right timing, to run away from the community!

Nevertheless, the Risen Jesus met them on the way and walked with them. In their hopelessness and disappointment, they did not recognize him: "Jesus said to them, 'What is this conversation which you are holding with each other as you walk?' And they stood still, looking sad . . . And they said to him, 'Concerning Jesus of Nazareth . . . But we had hoped that he was the one to redeem Israel'" (Lk 24:13-21). Because they felt lost with their hopes shattered, they decided to leave Jerusalem and go home and forget about it all! But Jesus manifested his glory to them both by opening their minds to the Scriptures and by breaking bread with them (Lk 24:27, 30-32).

It was like a new version of the glory of the Lord resting on the tabernacle and on the disciples encamped by the presence of the Lord (Num 9:15-16): "Their eyes were opened and they recognized him, and he vanished out of their sight . . . And they rose that same hour and returned to Jerusalem" (Lk 24:31-33). Having encamped by the Lord's presence, having listened to his word and broken bread with him, the glory of the Lord was then lifted up, and Jesus vanished from their sight.

The disciples then realized that they had made a mistake, they had not waited for the Lord to rise from the dead, and what was more, they had separated themselves from the community and moved away from Jerusalem. They returned "that same hour" (though evening had fallen and it was dark) to Jerusalem and to the community, with their hearts burning within them.

(2) The Joy of encamping in God's presence. This happened in the Old Testament, and it happens again and again in the New. An example comes to mind: Jesus is in Capernaum with his disciples when,

> *John's disciples and the Pharisees were fasting; and the people came and said to Jesus, "Why do John's disciples and the disciples of the Pharisees fast, but your disciples do not fast?" And Jesus said to them, "Can the wedding guests fast while the bridegroom is with them? As long as they have the bridegroom with them, they cannot fast. The days will come, when the bridegroom is taken away from them, and then they will fast in that day" (Mk 2:1, 18-20).*

When the bride and bridegroom are together at the wedding ceremony, everyone rejoices and they cannot mourn at that time. Jesus is the Bridegroom and we, the people of God, are together the Bride of Christ. St. Paul writes, "I betrothed you to Christ to present you as a pure bride to her one husband" (2 Cor 11:2). When wedding festivities are in progress, no one wants it to end. They want to stay and celebrate forever.

It must have been like that in the days of Moses when the people encamped in the desert whenever and wherever the glory of the Lord settled over the Tent of Meeting. That was the sign that the Lord was present, and that it was time to stop and celebrate with the Lord. God provided the food and the drink, God spoke the words they were to live by, especially in rough times. It was these days of encamping in the Lord's presence that provided the motivation and the energy to go on again on their journey to the Promised Land. When the Lord is present, everything becomes meaningful, bright and hopeful.

Jesus was explaining this joyful mystery to the people and the Pharisees, who could not understand why Jesus and his disciples did not observe fast days. They had not believed in the truth of

Jesus Christ. Jesus the Bridegroom was present, how could the Bride fast? "Let us rejoice and exult and give him the glory, for the marriage of the Lamb has come, and his Bride has made herself ready" (Rev 19:7).

Jesus, who is "the same yesterday and today and forever" (Heb 13:8), was pointing to the reality that was to come in the future, but the Pharisees' eyes were limited to the vision of the present and all they could think of and appreciate was the strict observance of the law. The one called John, to whom the revelation of Jesus Christ was given, tells us,

> Then I saw a new heaven and a new earth; for the first heaven and the first earth had passed away, and the sea was no more. And I saw the holy city, the new Jerusalem, coming down out of heaven from God, prepared as a bride adorned for her husband. And I heard a loud voice from the throne saying, "Behold, the dwelling of God is with mortals. He will dwell with them, and they shall be his people, and God himself will be with them; he will wipe away every tear from their eyes" (Rev 21:1-4).

Such is the joy of the moment of encamping and staying with the Lord in prayer and fellowship, celebrating the Lord's presence and becoming like him through his love and wisdom poured out in that moment. God calls you and me today saying,

> Be still and know that I am God! I am exalted among the nations, I am exalted in the earth! (Ps 46:10).

The Book of Deuteronomy

In this section, we contemplate Jesus as we dwell on passages taken mainly from the book of Deuteronomy. As we read them, let us appreciate Moses, the great prophet and deliverer, chosen by God for his people, and also listen carefully to what Jesus the Lord teaches and asks us to do.

Jesus and Moses

(1) The Lord God said to Moses,

> *I will raise up for them* a prophet like you *from among their brethren; and* I will put my words in his mouth, *and he shall speak to them all that I commanded him. (Deut 18:18, emphasis added).*

Moses conveys this promise of God to the people of Israel, saying, "The LORD your God will raise up for you *a prophet like me* from among you — him you shall heed" (Deut 18:15).

This promise was perfectly and definitively fulfilled in Jesus Christ. As we read through the pages of the Gospel accounts we hear Jesus proclaiming the Good News of the Kingdom of God, teaching, preaching, correcting, healing and speaking with the words that the Father put in his mouth. God had promised, "I will put my words in his mouth." Moses himself bears witness to Jesus Christ, who is the prophet *par excellence.*

> *When the people saw the sign which Jesus had done (multi-plication of the loaves and the fish), they said, "This is indeed the prophet who is to come into the world!" (Jn 6:14).*

Moses prefigures Jesus, the "prophet like me," whose coming he foretold. The first Christian martyr, Stephen, recalled this prophecy of Moses (Acts 7:37), and St. Peter proclaimed its ful-fillment in Jesus Christ (Acts 3:22).

Jesus too reminds the unbelieving Jews of the prophecy made by Moses about him, saying,

> *Do not think that I shall accuse you to the Father; it is Moses who accuses you, on whom you set your hope. If you believed Moses, you would believe me, for he wrote of me. But if you do not believe Moses' writings, how will you believe my words? (Jn 5:45-46).*

Through the mediation of his faithful servant Moses, God gave the Law only to the people of Israel, but through the mediation of Jesus, the new Moses, the new law and power of love, that is the Holy Spirit himself, has been poured out on all peoples. Through his Son Jesus Christ (1 Tim 2:4f), God now wants to save all of humankind, indeed the whole of creation. The letter to the Hebrews tells us,

> *Now Moses was faithful in all God's house as a servant, to tes-tify to the things that were to be spoken later, but Christ was faithful over God's house as a son. And we are his house if we hold fast our confidence and pride in our hope (Heb 3:5-6).*

As John's Gospel puts it, "The Law indeed was given through Moses; grace and truth came through Jesus Christ" (Jn 1:17).

Again, Moses told the people of Israel, "The LORD has sent me to do all these works; it has not been of my own accord" (Num 16:28). Moses, the humblest and most powerful among the prophets of God, whom the Lord called, "my servant Moses" (Num 12:7, 8), gave testimony to the fact that whatever he did and said was given to him from God, and not from his own authority.

Jesus, the humblest Servant of God, who being God did not grasp at divine glory and at equality with God, witnessed to the Father, saying,

> *The words that I say to you I do not speak on my own author-*
> *ity; but the Father who dwells in me does his works... Very*
> *truly I tell you, the Son can do nothing on his own, but only*
> *what he sees the Father doing.... I can do nothing on my*
> *own... I seek to do not my own will but the will of him who*
> *sent me (Jn 14:10; 5:19, 30).*

Moses was chosen from among the people of Israel and sent by God with a unique mission for his people, and God often witnessed to the special choice and mission of Moses before the people of Israel: "My servant Moses... is entrusted with all my house. With him I speak face to face clearly, and not in riddles; and he beholds the form of the LORD" (Num 12:6-8).

Jesus was the Word made flesh, Emmanuel. He was not chosen from among other human beings but came from God. The Father sent Jesus to us because of his great love for us. The fourth Gospel insists: "God so loved the world that he gave his only Son" (Jn 3:16). Jesus came not just to liberate us from physical slavery, but indeed to give us a whole new life. Jesus said, "as Moses lifted up the serpent in the wilderness, so must the Son of man be lifted up, that whoever believes in him may have eternal life" (Jn 3:14-15).

All this was confirmed by the fact that Moses was one of the two Old Testament representatives who appeared at Jesus' side at the Transfiguration (Lk 9:30f).

Jesus Christ surpasses the Law by fulfilling it. Jesus is indeed the end of the old Law, as Paul points out, "For Christ is the end of the law, that every one who has faith may be justified" (Rom 10:4). Having accomplished all that was written of him in the Law of Moses, God raised Jesus from the dead in order to give the Holy Spirit to all who thirst (Lk 24:44-49).

(2) There is a strong connection between the Father and his Son, and between Jesus and the Father and us. This relationship of loving union remains strong and unbreakable through the word of God. We are called to *heed*, "listen to" the word that God speaks. God the Father commands us to listen to Jesus.

A good example: Jesus "took Peter and James and John, and led them up a high mountain apart . . . there he was transfigured before them" (Mt 17:1-2), and "a bright cloud overshadowed them," and the voice of the Father was heard. He declared, "This is my beloved Son, with whom I am well pleased, listen to him" (Mt 17:5).

So all that matters, and all that is needed, is our heeding the word, which means detaching ourselves from so many other words and sounds from inside and outside us.

We can see both Moses and Jesus constantly detaching themselves from the crowds and the disciples, and going to a lonely place, often to a mountain-top, only to commune with God. In that time of prayer and communication, Moses received all the words that he was to speak to the people, and the power to work wonders among them. When God called Moses to go and speak to Pharaoh and liberate his people from the bondage of slavery and oppression in Egypt, Moses made many excuses to avoid being sent. One of the many excuses he made was, "O my Lord, I have never been eloquent, neither in the past nor even now that you have spoken to your servant; but I am slow of speech and slow of tongue" (Ex 4:10). And yet we see the same Moses, of course older and wiser in the book of Deuteronomy, speaking with authority and confidence saying: "You shall put *these words of mine* in your heart and soul ... diligently observe this entire commandment that I am commanding you ... No one will be able to stand against you" (Deut 11:18-25, emphasis added).

We see Jesus too speaking to the disciples and the crowds, especially in the Sermon on the Mount (Mt 5:7). The Evangelists tell us that Jesus spoke with authority. Jesus announced to his hearers,

> *Every one then who hears* these words of mine *and does them will be like a wise man who built his house upon a rock ... And when Jesus finished these sayings, the crowds were astonished at his teaching, for he taught them as one who had authority, and not as their scribes* (Mt 7:24-29).

Again and again we hear Jesus saying, "You have heard that it was said to those of ancient times ... *But I say to you* ... (Mt 5:21-22, 27-28, 31-32, 33-34, 38-39, 43-44, emphasis added). Jesus speaks with the authority of the Son of God, our Redeemer.

As disciples, we must regularly check to see whether we are diligently obeying all that we have heard from our Teacher and Savior, Jesus. This is the only way in which we can show our genuine love for the loving God. This is why we hear Moses saying to the people, "For the LORD your God is testing you, to know whether you love the LORD your God with all your heart and with all your soul. You shall walk after the LORD your God and keep his commandments and obey his voice, and ... cleave to him" (Deut 13:3-4).

Jesus said, "If you love me, you will keep my commandments"(Jn 14:15). In our daily lives too we can see that when we truly love somebody, we listen and act according to the likes and dislikes of the beloved one. When we love, then obedience flows from our heart. It is not a burden at all. But when the self comes in between and selfish desires block pure love, then obedience seems most difficult, and relationships get strained. Jesus reminds us, "You are my friends if you do what I command you" (Jn 15:14).

(3) Moses said to the people,

See, I have set before you today life and prosperity, death and adversity. If you obey the commandments of the LORD your God that I am commanding you today, by loving the LORD your God, walking in his ways, and observing his commandments, then you shall live . . . I have set before you life and death, blessings and curses. Choose life so that you may live (Deut 30:15-20).

Life and prosperity, death and adversity, all depend on whether we are leading a life motivated by self-giving love or selfish gratification. Life is made beautiful only when our lives can give life to others. Let us ask ourselves, first of all, are we believers in a loving God? If so, do we really love God in a response of gratitude and happiness? Godly love is not an abstract matter of philosophy, but a way of living day by day. Today, perhaps, we could check what kind of fruit our own lives have borne? Do I have inner peace of mind and joy in heart despite the difficulties and problems in my life? Walking diligently in the ways of the Lord brings such peace and joy, because they are borne out of our love for God and neighbor.

Jesus too explains how we can choose life and live fruitful lives in the sight of God and others. He teaches,

Enter by the narrow gate; for the gate is wide and the way is easy that leads to destruction, and those who enter by it are many. For the gate is narrow and the way is hard that leads to life, and those who find it are few (Mt 7:13-14).

This is a paradox. True life and prosperity can be achieved only by facing and overcoming adversity and entering through the narrow gate. It is not so easy to enter through a narrow door. We need to be slim and trim. Moreover, we must be careful to walk every step in faith, shedding away all the unwanted fat of self-seeking and worldly wisdom. Perhaps the experience of being trimmed or *pruned* is not so pleasurable, but the results are beautiful. Hence Jesus adds, "Every branch of mine that bears no fruit, my Father takes away, and every branch that does bear fruit he prunes, that it may bear more fruit" (Jn 15:2).

Becoming trim and experiencing pruning are difficult as long as the process is on, but if we keep our eyes on the goal then it becomes desirable and fulfilling. Observing the commandments of the Lord and walking in his footsteps is no easy matter, but let us take it one step at a time, making every effort to live by the word of God, and true happiness will be ours for sure. Jesus himself promised this when he said, "Because I live, you will live also" (Jn 14:19b).

(4) Moses recounted for the people the fact of God's loving Providence during all the forty years that they had to journey through the desert. God fed them with manna and gave them water to drink. He even took care of their clothing and footwear:

> *Remember the long way that the LORD your God has led you these forty years in the wilderness... The clothes on your back did not wear out and your feet did not swell these forty years (Deut 8:2, 4).*

For forty long years, the people of Israel had no chance to visit stores for new clothes and shoes, not even if it was a special day in their lives. Yet they lacked nothing. The Father took care of every need of theirs, food, clothing, shelter.

What are the implications for ourselves? For a moment let us pause here, dear Reader, and reflect on how many times we have gone shopping for clothes and shoes this very year? And how many old clothes, which may not fit today, are lying layer upon layer in our cupboards? Do we really need them? Probably most of us will agree that we do not need them for ourselves any more.

Therefore, sharing in the concern of God for the poor, could we not be generous and give away even some good clothes and good shoes that we do not wear anymore for whatever reason, to those who may never be able to afford them?

Jesus describes beautifully the loving care and generosity of God our Father, saying,

> *I tell you, do not worry about your life, what you will eat or what you will wear. Look at the birds of the air; they neither sow nor reap nor gather into barns, and yet your heavenly Father feeds them. Are you not of more value than they? And why do you worry about clothing? Consider the lilies of the field, how they grow; they neither toil nor spin, yet I tell you, even Solomon in all his glory was not clothed like one of these ... will he not much more clothe you, O you of little faith?* (Mt 6:25-30).

It is also true, I believe, that God gives abundantly to us so that we, in turn, may give generously to those in need. Moses said to the people, "For the poor will never cease out of the land; therefore I command you, open wide your hand to the needy and to the poor in the land" (Deut 15:11).

God has a soft spot for the needy. God's eyes are attracted to those who have little or nothing. Those who have little or nothing are the ones who are open to receiving from God and from us. We are called to share in this quality of God's goodness. Of course, we can never match God's generosity, for he does not give us leftovers, he only gives us the best. Great is the goodness of the Lord, it cannot be measured! Moses told the people, and Jesus tells his disciples yesterday and today, "Give to him who begs from you, and do not refuse him who would borrow from you" (Mt 5:42).

In another event of the Gospels, we come across a moment in the life of Jesus and the first disciples when *a woman came up to him with an alabaster flask of very expensive ointment, and she poured it on his head, as he sat at table. But when the disciples saw it, they were indignant, saying, "Why this waste? For this ointment might have been sold for a large sum, and given to the poor." But Jesus, aware of this, said to them, "Why do you trouble the woman? For she has done a beautiful thing to me. For you always have the poor with you, but you will not always have me"* (Mt 26:7-11).

This underscores both the need to devote some resources to honor and worship God, and the need to devote some resources for the uplift of the poor. The beautiful reward is in the knowledge that when we give to the poor and the needy, we are, in fact, also giving to Jesus who is Good News to the poor: "Truly, I say to you, as long as you did it to one of the least of these who are members of my family, you did it to me" (Mt 25:40).

(5) Moses had the compassionate heart of a true leader. He was concerned about the continuity of leadership after him. He wanted to have someone to succeed him, a person who would care for the people and teach and instruct them and lead them forward in God's ways. So he said to the Lord,

"Let the Lord, the God of the spirits of all flesh, appoint a man over the congregation, who shall go out before them and come in before them, who shall lead them out and bring them in; that the congregation of the Lord may not be as sheep which have no shepherd." *And the* Lord *said to Moses, "Take Joshua the son of Nun, a man in whom is the spirit, and lay your hand upon him . . . You shall invest him with some of your author-ity, that all the congregation of the people of Israel may obey"* (Num 27:16-20, emphasis added).

In like manner, Jesus was concerned that other human beings, especially the twelve apostles, and indeed every Christian of every generation, should share in and continue the mission given him by his Father. Jesus himself went about all the cities and villages, teaching and proclaiming the good news of the kingdom, and curing all the sick. A huge crowd along with some disciples always followed Jesus, listening to him, getting nourishment from the word of God preached by him, receiving healings and meaning for their lives.

> *When Jesus saw the crowds, he had compassion for them, because they were harassed and helpless, like sheep without a shepherd. Then he said to his disciples, "The harvest is plentiful, but the laborers are few; therefore* ask the Lord of the harvest to send out laborers into his harvest" *(Mt 9:36-38, emphasis added).*

Whereas Moses asked the Lord for a successor as shepherd for the flock and leader for the people, Jesus asks his disciples to pray to the Father to send out laborers (not one but many) into the harvest, leaders who would serve and gather in the people, care for them and lead them to the Lord of the harvest.

Jesus asked his disciples to pray and he himself "went out to the mountain to pray."

> *He spent the night in prayer to God. And when day came, he called his disciples and chose twelve of them, whom he also named apostles (Lk 6:12-16).*

The apostles were chosen and appointed by Jesus, they did not succeed Jesus as Joshua succeeded Moses. Later on in the Gospel accounts we see that Peter is chosen by Jesus as the leader of the apostles, and down the ages to our day, the bishops have succeeded the apostles. Jesus is the only begotten Son of God, and "to all who received him, who believed in his name, he gave power to become children of God" (Jn 1:12). The apostles were chosen from among the disciples to be with Jesus and to be sent out to proclaim the message of the Kingdom and to have authority over unclean spirits (cf. Mk 3:14-15).

The Lord had told Moses to give Joshua "some of your own authority so that the people may obey." So too, "Jesus called the twelve together and gave them power and authority" (Lk 9:1).

While investing the apostles with power and authority, Jesus promised the Holy Spirit. He told them before he ascended to the Father, "You will receive power when the Holy Spirit has come upon you; and you will be my witnesses . . . to the ends of the earth" (Acts 1:8). Hence, the mission of the twelve was not just to teach and preach but to be witnesses of Jesus before the Christian community and the whole world. Wherever they went with the power and authority of Jesus and the Holy Spirit, the result was that many people turned back to God, their loving Father.

(6) Moses warned the people against false prophets, who would arise even from among them, to seduce the people away from the true God and lead them to false gods. They would create confusion in the people's hearts and minds by their clever arguments and sensational works of wonder, and thereby they would take them away from their first love, the God who had made a covenant with them, and called and chosen them to be his own people (Deut 14:2). Moses warned the people with these words:

If a prophet arises among you, or a dreamer of dreams, and gives you a sign or a wonder, and the sign or wonder which he tells you comes to pass, and if he says, "Let us go after other gods," which you have not known, "and let us serve them," you shall not listen to the words of that prophet or to that dreamer of dreams (Deut 13:1-3).

Notice that Moses makes it very clear that the words and the works of false prophets are not consistent with the truth. Their works show one thing and their words say something else. Hence, clearly they are deceivers. Also, Moses says that it is possible that they will work signs and wonders, which in turn will be able to seduce the people away from the truth.

It has been the experience of the Church too that people, whose faith is weak, are more easily taken up by sensational signs and wonders, and easily fall prey to false prophets. Let us for a moment reflect and examine how committed we are to the truth and, whether our faith is based on a correct interpretation of the word of God, rather than on the novel interpretations of Scripture given by self-styled preachers and false prophets; many of these go about trying to prove their power by working signs and wonders that take us away from authentic discipleship and the Cross of Christ.

Jesus warned his disciples saying,

> *Beware of false prophets, who come to you in sheep's clothing but inwardly are ravenous wolves. You will know them by their fruits (Matt 7:15-16).*

Jesus minces no words while warning his disciples and his listeners about false prophets. He describes them clearly and even points to a very important element of discernment, namely, you know the worth of a tree by the fruit it bears. The words and works of the false prophets do not yield lasting and nourishing fruit. Their fruit grows fast and withers away like straw: "Every tree that does not bear good fruit is cut down and thrown into the fire. Thus you will know them by their fruits" (Mt 7:19-20).

We know and believe that Jesus is the Truth (Jn 14:6), and that the false prophets are liars and deceivers. Their words and works always go against the Truth. In fact they pose as the only ones with the truth and teach all kinds of false doctrines and practices. They sometimes even go so far as to pose as Jesus Christ himself. In our day too, we may come across such self-styled leaders and false prophets. Warning against such deceivers, Jesus said,

Take heed that you are not led astray; for many will come in my name, saying, "I am he!" and, "The time is at hand!" Do not go after them (Lk 21:8).

With this warning, Jesus also tells us what to do when we encounter such false prophets. We must not go after them or allow ourselves to be led astray by them. We need to ask the Holy Spirit to help us grow up to maturity in Christ, "so that we may no longer be children, tossed to and fro and carried about with every wind of doctrine, by the cunning of men, by their craftiness in deceitful wiles" (Eph 4:14).

And many false prophets will arise and lead many astray . . . and because wickedness is multiplied, most people's love will grow cold. But the ones who endure to the end will be saved (Mt 24:11-13).

(7) Moses spoke to the people about the Year of Liberty, saying,

At the end of every seven years you shall grant a remission of debts. And this is the manner of the remission: every creditor shall remit the claim that is held against a neighbor, not exacting it of his neighbor, because the LORD's remission has been proclaimed . . . There will be no one in need among you (Deut 15:1-4).

This command of Moses was drawn from the command that the Lord God had given him on Mount Sinai:

In the seventh year there shall be a sabbath of complete rest for the land . . . You shall count off seven weeks of years, seven times seven years, so that the period of seven weeks of years

gives forty nine years. Then you shall have the trumpet sounded loud; on the tenth day of the seventh month — on the day of atonement — you shall have the trumpet sounded ... and you shall hallow the fiftieth year and proclaim liberty throughout the land to all its inhabitants. It shall be a jubilee for you: you shall return, every one of you, to your property and every one of you to your family.

When you make a sale ... you shall not cheat ... Do not take interest when you lend money ... Slaves shall serve you until the year of jubilee. Then they and their children shall be free from your authority (Lev 25:8-41).

The qualities with which the Year of Jubilee was seasoned were freedom, liberty, joy, fellowship, equality, reconciliation, and love. "God is love" (1 Jn 4:8). And God delights in the love his children have for one another. When recriminations and divisions take hold of the people, God gives them fresh opportunities to return to love and friendship. This seems to be the motive for the Year of Jubilee when debts were forgiven, slaves set free, property returned and there was to be no one in need in the land. It was a time for rejoicing when all equally enjoyed food, shelter, clothing, freedom, and dignity.

However, we human beings are often stubborn and hardhearted. Having received so much from God at every step of our lives, directly and through others, we still remain ungrateful and selfish, and look more and more for self-gratification. Again and again God wants to change our self-centered hearts and pleads with us to listen to him. The psalmist tells us poignantly with what words the Lord God pleads with his people:

Listen, my people to my warning, O Israel, if only you would heed! ... O that my people would heed me, that Israel would walk in my ways! (Ps 81:8-13).

But again and again the Old Testament records how God's people failed him. So, in his love and mercy, God himself found a way to make the people heed his voice and walk in his ways. When the time was right, God sent his only begotten Son, Jesus. He is the Way that God gave for us (Jn 14:6). After completing the forty days of his fasting and conquering every temptation of the enemy, Jesus came to Nazareth at the beginning of his public ministry. He entered the synagogue on the sabbath and stood up to read. The reading of the day was from the prophet Isaiah. Jesus unrolled the scroll and found the place where it was written,

> *The Spirit of the Lord is upon me, because he has anointed me to bring good news to the poor. He has sent me to proclaim release to the captives and recovery of sight to the blind, to let the oppressed go free, to proclaim the year of the Lord's favor (Lk 4:18-19; Is 61:1-2a).*

Jesus not only proclaimed *the year of the Lord's favor*, in his own Person he ushered it in definitively. With Jesus has come the year of liberty, the time of salvation. The words of the prophet Isaiah were perfectly fulfilled in Jesus Christ, as he himself declared to those present, "Today this scripture has been fulfilled in your hearing" (Lk 4:21).

Jesus is good news to the poor. Wherever he is, light and life go before him. In his presence, and by his words and deeds, every oppressed person is set free, and every one in need is satisfied. Jesus sets free all those in any kind of bondage, he speaks his word and it accomplishes all that he says.

When John's disciples came to ask Jesus whether he was the promised Messiah, Jesus responded by pointing out all that had been accomplished by him.

> *Jesus answered them, "Go and tell John what you hear and see: the blind receive their sight and the lame walk, lepers are*

cleansed and the deaf hear, the dead are raised up, and the poor
have good news preached to them" (Mt 11:4-5).

Whereas Jesus can accomplish all things by himself, yet, he
desires that we become his partners in his work of salvation. He
sets us free so that we can become laborers in the work of freedom
of all peoples. He gives us power to do whatever he did. This
power is the Holy Spirit. Jesus says,

As the Father has sent me, even so I send you (Jn 20:21).

Go into all the world and preach the gospel to the whole cre-
ation (Mk 16:15).

You shall receive power when the Holy Spirit has come upon
you; and you shall be my witnesses . . . to the ends of the earth
(Acts 1:8; Lk 24:48-49).

Jesus wants us to heed his words and obey them. He says, "If
you continue in my word, you are truly my disciples, and you will
know the truth, and the truth will make you free" (Jn 8:31-32).

What is our own response when we hear these words of Jesus?
Are we ready to give up our own prejudices and resentments first
and become witnesses of forgiveness, reconciliation and freedom
in the Holy Spirit? When we do whatever he tells us, then God can
enable us to bring the good news of freedom and liberty to all
human beings, even to the whole of creation,

For the creation waits with eager longing for the revealing of
the children of God . . . because the creation itself will be set
free from its bondage to decay and obtain the glorious liberty
of the children of God (Rom 8:21).

(8) Moses said to the people,

This commandment which I command you this day is not too hard for you, neither is it far off. It is not in heaven, that you should say, "Who will go up for us to heaven, and bring it to us, that we may hear it and do it?" Neither is it beyond the sea, that you should say, "Who will go over the sea for us, and bring it to us, that we may hear it and do it?" But the word is very near you; it is in your mouth and in your heart, so that you can do it (Deut 30:11-14).

"The word is very near you." Moses heard and taught the spoken word of God. He could see the glory of God, even if only dimly, and hear the word whenever God's voice came to him. Moses was the beloved of and close to the Lord God, but even he had not beheld the glory of the personified Word of God. How truly blessed *we* are to have known the Word of God in Person. Jesus is this Word of God. He said to his disciples,

Blessed are your eyes, for they see, and your ears, for they hear. Truly, I say to you, many prophets and righteous men longed to see what you see, and did not see it, and to hear what you hear, and did not hear it (Mt 13:16-17).

The fourth Gospel declares this profound truth in its Prologue. We read,

In the beginning was the Word, and the Word was with God, and the Word was God ... And the Word became flesh and dwelt among us, full of grace and truth; we have beheld his glory, glory as of the only Son from the Father (Jn 1:1, 14).

Jesus is the Son of the Father who brings the word closer and nearer by his presence, and in his words and deeds. He is the Word who has both descended from heaven and also ascended into heaven.

No one has ascended into heaven but he who descended from heaven, the Son of man (Jn 3:13).

The word was not far from the people of Israel, as Moses had pointed out, it was on their lips and in their hearts. They recited and repeated the word and believed in the word and obeyed it.

The word is closer to us now than it ever was, in the Person of Jesus Christ the Savior. All we have to do is to listen to him and imitate him. Children learn by imitation, and Jesus tells us to become like little children (Mt 18:3). Jesus obeyed the will of God perfectly. By keeping the word in our hearts and acting according to the word, we will also do what Jesus did, and be loved by the Father. Jesus said to the disciples and he says to us today,

If a person loves me, he will keep my word, and my Father will love him, and we will come to him and make our home with him. He who does not love me does not keep my words; and the word which you hear is not mine but the Father's who sent me (Jn 14:23-24).

The connection between God and us, or Jesus and us, is so clearly held together by the word of God (see no. 2 above). Therefore, let us open our hearts to the Word of God today, that we may always enjoy the love and fellowship of the Holy Spirit who inspires the word of God at every moment.

(9) The Deuteronomist ends the book with these words in praise of Moses,

Never since has there arisen a prophet in Israel like Moses, whom the LORD knew face to face. He was unequalled . . . for all the mighty deeds and all the terrifying displays of power that Moses performed in the sight of all Israel (Deut 34:10-12).

God is the glory of all his chosen ones. God makes his servants powerful and fruitful. Although God does all the works of power and glory, yet the servants of the Lord are given praise and glory for having been good instruments of the Lord. The faithful servants of the Lord are always remembered by generations to come. Moses was an "unequalled" servant of the Lord through whom God worked mighty wonders and delivered his people from slavery and protected them through the wilderness for forty years. God gave his commandments through Moses. Whenever any instruction was to be given or a declaration to be made, God would give Moses the words to speak and the words were full of power and splendor.

The fourth Gospel likewise ends with words which speak about the unparalleled magnitude of Jesus' words and works:

There are also many other things that Jesus did; if every one of them were written down, I suppose that the world itself could not contain the books that would be written (Jn 21:25).

For more than two thousand years the same story and teachings and works of Jesus have been read, narrated and written about. And yet the name of Jesus always holds attention and exudes newness. Jesus remains forever new, his words remain forever life-giving, his death and resurrection remains forever the greatest work of salvation, which no one has ever repeated or can ever repeat.

Jesus Christ ... completed and perfected Revelation and confirmed it with divine guarantees. He did this by the total fact of his presence and self-manifestation by words and works, signs and miracles, but above all by his death and glorious resurrection from the dead, and finally by sending the Spirit of truth ... and no new public revelation is to be expected before the glorious manifestation of our Lord, Jesus Christ (Vatican II, *Dei Verbum*, n.4).

Jesus is the greatest human being that ever lived on earth. His greatness comes directly from heaven, for he is the Son of God. In the times when Jesus communed with the Father, he too knew the Father face to face. And what was more, in Jesus the face of the Father was perfectly reflected for all to see. This is possible because Jesus tells us, "the Father is in me and I am in the Father," and "I and the Father are one" (Jn 10:38,30).

In Jesus is completed all that the Lord God ever desired for his people. God has come close to his people forever, as a Father to his children, in and through Jesus. Therefore, haven't we the responsibility in turn to come closer to God our Father, and reflect his grace to others? St. James tells us how to do that:

> *God opposes the proud, but gives grace to the humble. Submit yourselves therefore to God. Resist the devil and he will flee from you. Draw near to God and he will draw near to you* (Jas 4:6-8).

SEEKING JESUS...
In the Psalms

The Psalms

Speaking about the book of Psalms, St. Ambrose declared that Jesus was the One whom the psalmists were announcing in the psalms. He said,

> What other prophets announced in enigmas seems to have been promised quite openly to the psalmist alone, namely that the Lord Jesus would be born of David's seed, as the Lord told him: "One of the sons of your body I will set on your throne" (Ps 132:11).
>
> In the book of the Psalms, not only is Jesus born for us: he accepts too his saving passion, he dies, he rises from the dead and ascends into heaven and sits at the Father's right hand. This prophet alone (the psalmist) announced what no other had dared to say, and what was later preached in the gospel by the Lord himself.

I discovered the truth of St. Ambrose's words while praying the psalms every day in the Liturgy of the Hours. In the psalms, we can both hear Jesus praying the psalms himself, and hear the psalmist speaking out loud about the promised Messiah who would fulfill all the promises made by God. In the life, words and works of Jesus, we can experience the psalms lived out perfectly by the one who was "greater than Solomon" in all his wisdom, and "greater than Jonah" in all his salvific preaching, dying, and rising from the dead. Indeed, we can truly "seek and find" Jesus in the psalms.

The psalms are the cries of the heart, prayers that were composed and sung many centuries before Jesus was born. The book of psalms contains the cries of several inspired psalmists, still it is King David, who lived around 1000 years before Christ, who was called "the sweet psalmist of Israel" and to whom the book of Psalms is attributed (2 Sam 23:1).

Jesus himself prayed and sang the psalms, for he was familiar with the Hebrew Scriptures (now called the Old Testament). We are specifically told that Jesus and his disciples prayed the psalms together after the Last Supper: "After psalms had been sung they left for the Mount of Olives" (Mt 26:30).

In this section of our reflections I invite you, dear Reader, to ask the Holy Spirit to reveal to you the face of Jesus more profoundly in the psalms. Not paying attention to the inadequacies of my words and insights, I pray that you will open the Bible and read the psalms prayerfully, making them a part of your own daily prayer. May you be drawn to pray the psalms in your everyday life and discover the Lord's magnificent beauty and power in them.

Another practical way you can pray the psalms every day by yourself and, at the same time, also join in prayer with the whole universal Church, is by obtaining a book of the Liturgy of the Hours, also called the Divine Office. The praying of the psalms, especially in the morning and the evening, and at other hours of the day, hallows every hour of the day. Down through the centuries, the Church has prayed in this manner from the Divine Office, and in the present times more and more lay men and women in the Catholic Church are making it their own way of praying the Scriptures, in union with the whole Church.

May God be gracious to us and bless us, and make his face to shine upon us (Ps 67:1).

PSALM 1

Blessed is the man who walks not in the counsel of the wicked . . . but his delight is in the law of the LORD, and on his law he meditates day and night . . . In all that he does, he prospers (Ps 1:1-3).

These lines of the psalm could very well be applied to Jesus! The Gospel accounts tell us how Jesus delighted in the word of God and constantly received counsel from it. Psalm 119:24,97 echoes what Jesus must have repeatedly said to the Father: "Your decrees (words) are my delight, they are my counselors. O, how I love your law (word)! It is my meditation all day long."

As the "Holy and Righteous One" (Acts 3:14), Jesus' delight was in the word of the Lord, and he meditated on God's word night and day, during his thirty or more years of "hidden life" in Nazareth, as well as his perhaps three years of public ministry in Galilee and Judea. Hence, whenever he spoke, his words were full of power to accomplish whatever he said. People were amazed and transformed when they listened to him, for "he taught them as one who had authority, and not as the scribes" (Mk 1:22).

Many a time, the power of Jesus' spoken word was drawn from the power of God's written word in Sacred Scripture. One example is how Jesus quelled the attacks and temptations of the devil in the desert after his days and nights of fasting in the wilderness. Just before Jesus went into the desert to fast and pray for forty days, he was baptized by John in the river Jordan. God's voice from the opened heavens had declared, "You are my beloved Son, in whom I am well pleased" (Lk 3:21-22). Jesus is God's only begotten Son and at the same time he is human just like you and me. Hence Jesus could and did experience temptation, just as we do (Heb.4:15).

More importantly, the way that Jesus responded to temptation shows us how we too can do the same. Although he was tempted like us, he did not fall. The tempter challenged the fact of Jesus' divine sonship, urging him to *prove* it by using his special relationship with God to his own advantage, that is, by changing the stones into bread to satisfy his stomach's hunger.

Jesus overcame this sly temptation by quoting the truth contained in the word of God: "It is written, 'Man shall not live by bread alone, but by every word that proceeds from the mouth of God'" (Mt 4:3-4; Deut 8:3).

Another temptation was about having for himself all the power and glory of this world, if only Jesus would first "fall down and worship" the devil. Jesus responded to the evil tempter, "Begone Satan! For it is written, 'You shall worship the Lord your God and him alone shall you serve'" (Mt 4:8-10; Deut 6:13).

Often in our lives, especially in these times of material consumerism, worldly pleasures and power, we too may be faced with such temptations. As devoted disciples of Jesus, we can learn from him, and always choose the values that Jesus himself gave us. Thus we will effectively repel the temptations of this world, the flesh, and the devil.

The proud tempter could not accept defeat so easily from Jesus, and he did not give up at once. He noticed that Jesus had so far defeated him by using an effective weapon: "the sword of the Spirit, which is the word of God" (Eph 6:17). Hence, the tempter continued to try further, this time "using" scripture to try to deceive Jesus. He quoted from Ps 91:11-12, saying, "Throw yourself down (from the pinnacle of the temple), for it is written, 'He will give his angels charge of you.'"

An important principle of interpreting Sacred Scripture is that a text of Scripture must never be taken out of its whole context to be made into a pretext for one's selfish convenience. This is what the devil was doing then, and continues to do even today with the disciples of Jesus. We need to recognize this temptation and overcome it by making time each day, or a longer time once a week, to become *familiar* with Sacred Scripture. Psalm 91 is about God's protection for the one who trusts in God, who loves and knows his name.

> *He who dwells in the shelter of the Most High, who abides in the shadow of the Almighty, will say to the LORD, "My refuge and my fortress; my God, in whom I trust. . . . Because you have made the LORD your refuge, the Most High your habitation, no evil shall befall you . . . for he will give his angels charge of you to guard you in all your ways. On their hands they will bear you up, lest you dash your foot against a stone . . . Because he cleaves to me in love, I will deliver him"* (Ps 91:1-14a).

The psalm describes well the real qualities of Jesus and his Father. Yet, the tempter used the very words of the psalm to try to deceive Jesus! Can the devil ever tolerate any person walking in the way of the Lord or one who loves the Lord? Would he ever want us to do the will of God our Father? Never! In fact, it is the devil's main job to seduce and confuse us by twisting the truth. Thus he pressurizes us "to prove our worth" by doing just the opposite of what we ought to do as God's children. He tried to do this with Jesus too. He twisted Scripture to suit his own purpose of allurement. He quoted the Bible to taunt and provoke Jesus to enter into a discussion with him. Using crafty reasoning, the devil thought that he would be able to make Jesus fall. But Jesus knew the word of God well, and so could not be trapped by the devil's false reasoning or quoting out-of-context.

The serpent had used the same trick to lead Eve into sin. She entered into unnecessary conversation with the devil, and was soon deceived. It may have seemed quite a sensible and profitable discussion to her, but only later did she sadly realize that its result was separation from the loving God who had created her for a life of beauty and happiness.

Let us look more in detail at what happened in Eve's temptation. The crafty serpent did not straight away tempt Eve to eat of the fruit of the forbidden tree. Rather he asked her a provocative question,

Did God say, "You shall not eat from any tree in the garden?" The woman said to the serpent, "We may eat of the fruit of the trees in the garden; but God said, you shall not eat of the fruit of the tree that is in the middle of the garden, nor shall you touch it, or you shall die." But the serpent said to the woman, "You will not die; for God knows that when you eat of it your eyes will be opened, and you will be like God, knowing good and evil." So . . . she took the fruit and ate (Gen 3:1-6).

It could be the same situation with us too, for we do not take the trouble to discern the use of the word of God that comes from lying tongues and so we often fall. Let us ask Jesus for the grace to overcome such evil temptations where the tempter uses words from Scripture to make us fall. St. Paul warns us, saying,

The time is coming when people will not put up with sound doctrine, but having itching ears, they will accumulate for themselves teachers to suit their own desires, and will turn away from listening to the truth (2 Tim 4:3-4).

When the tempter provoked Jesus to claim the words of the psalm and jump from the pinnacle, Jesus replied, "Again it is written, 'You shall not tempt the Lord your God'" (Mt 4:5-7; Deut 6:16).

The Scriptures teach about Jesus, the Messiah, the Savior, the Son of Man (cf. Dan 7:13-14). He has the fullness of divine revelation within himself, and all that the Father has ever promised is fulfilled perfectly in Jesus. Therefore, when Jesus says a word taking it from Scripture, it is always within the context. Peter likewise had to remind the early Christians about the perennial need for discernment, since even Paul's letters were being (and still are!) twisted and quoted out of context by false teachers:

> *Our beloved brother Paul wrote to you according to the wisdom given him — there are some things in them hard to understand, which the ignorant and the unstable twist to their own destruction, as they do the other scriptures. You therefore beloved, since you are forewarned, beware that you are not carried away with the error of the disobedient and lose your own stability (2 Pt 3:15-17, emphasis added).*

Jesus is the fruitful true Vine (Jn 15:1), who gives us the unfailing fruit of salvation. "All that he says and does prospers" (Ps 1:3), and is effective in our lives and in the life of all, for all times and seasons and generations. In contrast, the way and the word of the evil one always perishes (Ps 1:6).

Reflecting on all of this, we, the disciples of Jesus, have to make our choices:

- Do we want to walk by faith in Jesus, even though this way is not the easy and broad way? (see Mt 7:13-14).
- Do we choose to be led by the Spirit, accepting to be pruned in order that we may bear more fruit? (see Jn 15:2).
- Or do we wish to live a very comfortable, pampered, prosperous, lukewarm, but ever-dissatisfied worldly life in the present world, choosing the values of the Gospel only when *convenient?*

Let us remember that the narrow way leads to eternal life and the broad way leads to eternal ruin. Lord Jesus, help us to choose your way and live by your truth each day of our lives. Amen.

PSALMS 2 and 110

I would like to reflect here on two aspects of the psalmist's words, as we continue to seek the face of Jesus.

> (1) *Why do the nations conspire and the peoples plot in vain? The kings of the earth set themselves ... against the LORD and his anointed? ... Then he will speak to them ... saying, "I have set my king on Zion, my holy hill"* (Ps 2:1-6).

I can hear these words echoing in the background right through the trial of Jesus, as he stood before the bloodthirsty elders, the chief priest and the scribes of the Sanhedrin, in the courts of Pilate, and in the barracks of the mocking and violent soldiers.

Jesus was the Christ, the Anointed One (the Greek word "*Christos*" means "the anointed one," in Hebrew: "*Messias*"). Jesus, who was anointed by the Spirit of the Lord, was conceived by the same Holy Spirit in Mary's womb. Then the Spirit descended upon Jesus in public, in an action of anointing, as St. Luke tells us:

> *When Jesus also had been baptized, and was praying, the heaven was opened, and the Holy Spirit descended upon him ... and a voice came from heaven, "You are my beloved Son; with you I am well pleased"* (Lk 3:21-22).

Still later, when Jesus returned to Nazareth at the beginning of his public ministry, after the fasting and temptations, he confirmed that he was the one anointed by the Spirit:

> *And he came to Nazareth ... he went to the synagogue on the sabbath day. And he stood up to read; and there was given to him the book of the prophet Isaiah. He opened the book and found the place where it was written, "The Spirit of the Lord is upon me, because he has anointed me to preach good news to the poor ... to proclaim the acceptable year of the Lord."*

... And he began to say to them, "Today this scripture has been fulfilled in your hearing" (Lk 4:16-21; cf. Is 61:1-2a).

In the presence of all, Jesus declared that the time of waiting of the Jewish people was over, that God had fulfilled his promises of sending the anointed Messiah by his sending of Jesus, his Son. But the people did not believe him, in fact, they wanted to kill him right there.

The psalmist's words, "The LORD will speak to them (i.e. to the nations and the peoples who plot against the Lord's anointed), saying, 'I have set my king on Zion, on my holy hill'" are fulfilled in Jesus — he is the eternal king whose reign never ends and who is the "eternal high priest" set on the holy hill of God (cf. Heb 7:26; 9:11ff; etc.).

(2) *I will tell of the decree of the LORD: He said to me, "You are my son, today I have begotten you" (Ps 2:7).*

As Jesus rose from the dead and came out of the grave, we can imagine Jesus singing and affirming these words of the psalm: "I will tell of the decree of the Lord, my Father, who has said to me, 'You are my son, today I have begotten you'!"

This "begetting" refers not so much to the birth of Jesus in Bethlehem, but to his victorious rising from the dead, for Jesus is indeed, "the firstborn from the dead" (Col 1:18). St. Paul understood the words of the psalm in this sense when he proclaimed:

And we bring you the good news that what God promised to our ancestors he has fulfilled for us, their children, by raising Jesus; as also it is written in the second psalm, "You are my Son; today I have begotten you" (Acts 13:32-33).

This same message is contained in the prayer of Psalm 110:1:

The LORD says to my lord, "Sit at my right hand until I make your enemies your footstool."

St. Peter announced this truth to the crowds who had come to celebrate the fiftieth day after the Passover, called "Pentecost" in Jerusalem. At the sound of the rush of the wind (the Spirit), they gathered to listen to what Peter was saying as he declared confidently that these words of the psalm were not fulfilled in David, but in the one about whom David himself had spoken.

Fellow Israelites, I may say to you confidently of our ancestor David that he both died and was buried, and his tomb is with us to this day . . . David spoke of the resurrection of the Messiah . . . This Jesus God raised up, and of that all of us are witnesses.

Being therefore exalted at the right hand of God, and having received from the Father the promise of the Holy Spirit, he has poured out this that you both see and hear. For David did not ascend into the heavens, but he himself says, "The Lord said to my Lord, Sit at my right hand, until I make thy enemies a stool for your feet" (Acts 2:29-35).

By raising him from the dead, God established the eternal reign of Jesus, the King of kings. Jesus is the Son of God and the eternal King whose reign will never end. The Good News for us is that by the Holy Spirit, who is given as God's gift to those who believe, we too become sons and daughters of God in Jesus, and also co-heirs with Jesus in the eternal Kingdom. St. Paul explains this, saying,

For all who are led by the Spirit of God are children of God . . . you have received a spirit of adoption. When we cry, "Abba! Father!" it is the very Spirit bearing witness with our spirit that we are children of God and if children, then heirs, heirs

*of God and joint heirs with Christ if, in fact, we suffer with him
so that we may also be glorified with him (Rom 8:14-17).*

The above words of Paul point to a very important truth in the life of a disciple of Jesus. If we as branches are one with Jesus, who is the true Vine, it follows that because we share the same life of Jesus, we too will become fruitful branches, bearing fruit that will last. For this to happen, Jesus says, "My Father removes every branch in me that bears no fruit. Every branch that does bear fruit he prunes to make it bear more fruit" (Jn 15:1-2).

Pruning is the painful part of discipleship, but it has a purpose: that we may bear more fruit, fruit that will last.

So, it is up to us to choose whether we want to remain just nominal disciples or disciples who bear only minimal fruit, in which case someday we may find ourselves tired and shriveled up, ready to be broken off from the Vine; or whether we want to choose the life of the Spirit by denying our selfish motives and desires, and live for others and for the purpose for which God has given us life. If we choose the latter, then we will truly enjoy the fruits of the resurrection and be glorified with Jesus. Our lives will be worthwhile. Then we too will hear the voice from heaven declaring, "You are my child, my beloved, in whom I am well pleased."

PSALM 8

When I look at the heavens, the work of your hands, the moon and the stars which you have arranged, what is man that you are mindful of him, and the son of man that you care for him? Yet you have made him little less than God and crowned him with glory and honor. You have given him dominion over the works of your hands; you have put all things under his feet (Ps 8:3-6).

The letter to the Hebrews comments on some lines of this psalm. It says that more than to angels, it was to Jesus, the Son of Man, that God gave authority over all the works of his hands:

It was not to angels that God subjected the world to come. It has been testified somewhere, "what is man that you are mindful of him, or the son of man, that you care for him? You have made him for a little while lower than the angels, you have crowned him with glory and honor, putting everything in subjection under his feet."

Now in putting everything in subjection to him, he left nothing outside his control. As it is, we do not see everything in subjection to him. But we see Jesus, who for a little while was made lower than the angels, crowned with glory and honor because of the suffering of death, so that by the grace of God he might taste death for every one.

For it was fitting that he, for whom and by whom all things exist, in bringing many to glory, should make the pioneer of their salvation perfect through suffering (Heb 2:5-10).

St. Paul explains this mystery of Jesus' becoming "lower than the angels" and then being "crowned with glory and honor" in his famous hymn:

Though he was in the form of God . . . he emptied himself, taking the form of a servant, being born in the likeness of men . . . he humbled himself and became obedient unto death, even death on a cross.

Therefore God has highly exalted him . . . that at the name of Jesus every knee should bow, in heaven and on earth and under the earth, and every tongue confess that Jesus Christ is Lord, to the glory of God the Father (Phil 2:6-11).

It is the Father who crowned Jesus with glory and honor, and put all things under his care. Hence, it is to Jesus that all living creatures and angels sing their new song:

You are worthy . . . to receive power and wealth and wisdom and might and honor and glory and blessing forever and ever! Amen (Rev 5:9-14).

PSALM 16

(1) *"I bless the LORD who gives me counsel; in the night also, my heart instructs me" (Ps 16:7).*

Though at every moment of his life, Jesus was in communion with the Father, nevertheless in the Gospel accounts we very often find Jesus going away to deserted places to spend quality time with his Father in prayer. We are told that sometimes Jesus would stay up all night in prayer, especially when he had some very important decisions to make. He needed the counsel of the Father and the Spirit, and this required an intimate "consultation" or "listening," which in turn was possible only at night when all the crowds had gone away, or early in the morning. All day, from morning till night, Jesus had no time for himself, as St. Mark tells us: "The crowd came together again, so that they (Jesus and his disciples) could not even eat" (Mk 3:20).

The above-quoted words of Psalm 16:7 must have been whispered often by Jesus, and they are seen fulfilled perfectly in Jesus' life and ministry. St. Luke writes,

> *Now during those days Jesus went out to the mountain to pray; and he spent the night in prayer to God. And when day came, he called his disciples and chose twelve of them, whom he also named apostles (Lk 6:12f).*

Jesus chose the Twelve after a whole night in prayer, during which he was listening to God and experiencing deep communion with the Father and the Spirit. It was a critical moment in his ministry — out of so many disciples, Jesus had to choose just twelve, the number akin to the twelve tribes of Israel, and Jesus wanted to choose only those whom the Father had chosen. We know this from his own lips:

Very truly I tell you, the Son can do nothing on his own, but only what he sees the Father doing; for whatever the Father does, the Son does likewise. The Father loves the Son, and shows him all that he himself is doing . . . I can do nothing on my own (Jn 5:19f; 30).

Another instance (out of so many instances), where Jesus manifested clearly that he came to bring God's kingdom on earth and do only what God wanted him to do, was when after a whole day of preaching and healing, he went away alone to a deserted place:

While it was still very dark, Jesus got up and went out to a deserted place, and there he prayed . . . And Simon and his companions hunted for him. When they found him, they said to him, "Everyone is searching for you." Jesus answered, "Let us go on to the neighboring towns, so that I may proclaim the message there also; for that is what I came out to do" (Mk 1:35-38).

Simon Peter and the village people wanted Jesus to stay on in the same place and work more miracles for them. Perhaps it was the popularity and fame that attracted them: they would be able to have a mighty following and receive many favors for themselves if Jesus stayed on in Peter's house and continued his ministry from there.

But Jesus could not be tempted with sensational popularity and fame due to a mighty following of sign-seekers. He did only what the Father had sent him to do. Therefore, Jesus "would not entrust himself to them, because he knew all people, he himself knew what was in man" (Jn 2:24-25).

(2) I keep the LORD always before me; because he is at my right hand, I shall not be moved. Therefore my heart is glad and my soul rejoices; my body also rests secure. For you do not give me up to Sheol, or let your faithful one see the Pit. You show

me the path of life. In your presence there is fullness of joy, in your right hand are pleasures forevermore (Ps 16:8-11).

These words of the psalm foreshadow so well the trust that Jesus had in the Father's love and power. All during his life and ministry, Jesus surely prayed this psalm again and again with deep joy and confidence. Peter too must have prayed it often, because in his preaching about Jesus Christ the Savior, Peter quotes these verses of Psalm 16. He gives them a new interpretation in the light of the resurrection. Jesus had told his disciples, "The Holy Spirit, whom the Father will send in my name, will teach you everything, and remind you of all that I have said to you" (Jn 14:26). By the help of the Holy Spirit, Peter interprets these words of King David, the psalmist:

Jesus of Nazareth ... you crucified and killed ... But God raised him up ... because it was impossible for him to be held in its power. For David says concerning him, "I saw the Lord always before me, for he is at my right hand so that I will not be shaken, therefore my heart was glad, ... For you will not abandon my soul to Hades, or let your Holy One experience corruption" (Acts 2:22-28).

Peter continued,

I may say to you confidently of our ancestor David that he both died and was buried, and his tomb is with us to this day ... he knew that God had sworn that he would put one of his descendants on his throne. Foreseeing this, David spoke of the resurrection of the Messiah saying, "He was not abandoned to Hades, nor did his flesh experience corruption" (Ps 16:10). This Jesus God raised up, and of that all of us are witnesses (Acts 2:29-32).

The tomb could not hold Jesus, "the Author of life, whom God raised from the dead" (Acts 3:15). Let us too sing this psalm with the same confidence each day, as we share in the death and resurrection of Jesus through the various experiences of our lives, until we die and are raised again by the Father at the Coming of our Lord Jesus Christ.

PSALM 22

(1) *"My God, my God, why have you forsaken me?"* (Ps 22:1a).

This is one of the last words of Jesus from the cross. It is the most difficult one to understand because we believe that Jesus and the Father are one, and God the Father was always present to Jesus. But on the cross, Jesus cried out the opening words of this psalm in deep anguish and pain. The renowned biblical scholar, Fr. Raymond Brown, calls this "the death cry of Jesus." Jesus cried out "in a loud voice" to God.

Let us first recall the context: Jesus was abandoned by his disciples, arrested by the chief priests and soldiers, scourged and mocked by them and crucified mercilessly as a criminal, and now there was darkness over all the earth.

In such a situation, Jesus' cry is that of one who has actually plumbed the depths of the abyss of suffering. Jesus feels himself enveloped by the powers of darkness. Jesus, the Suffering Servant of God, the innocent and just One, cries out from the heart to God in the words of the psalm: "My God, my God, why have you forsaken me?"

If we reflect deeply on Jesus' situation here, we can almost feel Jesus' experience of the deep silence of God. Jesus cannot hear God speak words of consolation, he feels abandoned. And there is such darkness around him. The physical darkness is symbolic of the spiritual darkness of sin. On the cross, Jesus carries upon himself the sins of all humanity. It is in the nature of sin that it brings darkness and breaks relationship with God. Jesus who carried the sins of all of us and of all humanity upon himself on the cross, experienced loneliness and abandonment even from God his Father, the Holiest One, who cannot be found where sin exists.

The darkness caused by our sins is so penetrating for Jesus, that St. Paul tries to explain this profound mystery by writing, "For our sake God made him *to be sin*, who knew no sin." Jesus, who knew no sin, was made sin for you and me, "so that in him we might become the righteousness of God" (2 Cor 5:21). This is the limitless extent of the height and depth of God's love for us.

Notice the words Jesus uses here for the Father, whom he always called "Abba! Father!" From the cross Jesus cries out, "My God, my God. . . ." He addresses God in the way that all the people usually addressed God. On the cross, in that moment of loneliness because of the great barrier of our sins, Jesus felt utterly forsaken; he became "sin" to such an extent that he even gave up his usual intimate form of address for the Father.

> (2) But I am a worm, and not human; scorned by others, and despised by the people. All who see me mock at me; they make mouths at me, they shake their heads; "Commit your cause to the LORD; let him deliver — let him rescue the one in whom he delights!"
>
> . . . They stare and gloat over me; they divide my clothes among themselves, and for my clothing they cast lots (Ps 22:6-8; 17-18).

In the Gospel According to Matthew we read,

> When they had crucified him they divided his clothes among themselves by casting lots. Those who passed by derided him, shaking their heads and saying, "save yourself! If you are the Son of God, come down from the cross." In the same way the chief priests also, along with the scribes and elders, were mocking him, saying, "He saved others; he cannot save himself . . . let him come down from the cross now, and we will believe in him. He trusts in God; let God deliver him now, if he wants to; for he said, I am God's Son." The criminals who were crucified with him also taunted him in the same way (Mt 27:35, 39-44).

It is striking to note how the psalmist's words, written so many years before the birth of Jesus, are perfectly fulfilled in all that Jesus suffered from the people, the soldiers, the chief priests and the scribes at the time of his crucifixion. I believe that this was the moment when the enemy of Jesus, who had tempted him in the wilderness after Jesus' fasting, came back and attacked Jesus again with taunts, this time from the mouths of the chief priests and scribes and those who passed by.

Notice the tone of their words. They speak with such venom. Jesus, who had been through such terrible agony — hungry, thirsty, scourged — carried the heavy cross to Calvary, was stripped of his garments, nailed to the cross, and was now hanging on it as a criminal, had to listen to their blasphemous words of taunting and mocking. What was even more painful was the fact that they were even taunting God, the Father, whose loving will it was that Jesus, his beloved Son, should suffer all the agony and passion and crucifixion, to bring salvation to all, including his persecutors.

They said, "He trusts in God, let God deliver him now, if he wants to." This was a moment of seeming victory for the enemy of God who must have gleefully savored every moment when Jesus was cruelly tried, tortured, and finally nailed to the cross until death.

> Yet, Jesus laid down his life to fulfill God's loving plan. "God is Love" (1 Jn 4:8). The Gospel insists: "God loved the world so much that he gave his only Son . . . Indeed, God did not send the Son into the world to condemn the world, but in order that the world might be saved through him" (Jn 3:16-17).

The purpose of Jesus' death on the cross was our salvation and fullness of life. And "the last enemy to be destroyed is death" (1 Cor 15:26). By accepting death on the cross, Jesus destroyed death and restored life. This is why the same psalm says,

Posterity will serve him; future generations will be told about the LORD, *and proclaim his deliverance to a people yet unborn, saying that he has done it (Ps 22:30-31).*

When "God raised him up" from the dead, the enemy was totally defeated. All the sting of death was removed and sin was utterly defeated, and new hope, new faith and new love have now been given by Jesus to us who believe. We can all cry out now with full voice,

Death has been swallowed up in victory. Where, O death, is your victory? Where, O death, is your sting? Thanks be to God, who gives us the victory through our Lord Jesus Christ (1 Cor 15:54b-57).

PSALM 23

(1) *"The* LORD *is my shepherd, I shall not want"* (Ps 23:1).

We can echo this first verse of Psalm 23 in our hearts only if we trust in the Lord. A line in the book of Proverbs declares, "Trust in the Lord with all your heart, and do not rely on your own understanding" (Prov 3:5). Fear is a natural feeling, but we can overcome it by trusting in Jesus and his words. Many a time, the disciples of Jesus gave in to fear. But each time they heard Jesus challenge them not to be afraid and to trust in him. They had not yet learnt to apply the words of this psalm to their relationship with Jesus, "The LORD is my shepherd, I shall not want."

Let us recall a few examples of such incidents:

The disciples were afraid of ghosts. When Jesus came to them walking on the sea, they were terrified, thinking that a ghost was approaching them. But Jesus said to them, "Take heart, it is I; have no fear" (Mt 14:25-27).

To Jairus and his wife, whose daughter had died and whom Jesus would raise from the dead, Jesus said, "Do not fear; only believe" (Lk 8:50).

When the disciples were anxious about their future, because they had given up everything to follow Jesus, Jesus responded, "Fear not, little flock, for it is your Father's good pleasure to give you the kingdom" (Lk 12:32).

When the disciples were terrified because of the storm in the sea, Jesus "rebuked the wind and said to the sea, 'Peace! Be still!' And the wind ceased, and there was a great calm. He said to the disciples, 'Why are you afraid? Have you no faith?'" (Mk 4:39-40)

Jesus spoke to the disciples and said, "Peace I leave with you; my peace I give to you; not as the world gives do I give to you. Let not your hearts be troubled, neither let them be afraid" (Jn 14:27).

There are so many more instances in the Bible where the Father and Jesus repeatedly tell us not to be afraid, because the Lord God is with us to take care of us in whatever situation we find ourselves. Hence, the first words of Psalm 23 must become our daily prayer. Yes, the Lord is our Shepherd, we shall never be in want. We shall not lack any good thing while we live, and even when we die, our faith, hope, and love will see us transformed by his resurrection.

Jesus said, "I am the good shepherd . . . I lay down my life for my sheep" (Jn 10:11-15). It is for us that Jesus lays down his life, to take it up again (Jn 10:17). If Jesus gives his life for us, what more can we ask for?

(2) "He makes me lie down in green pastures; he leads me beside still waters; he restores my soul" (Ps 23:2-3).

Jesus provides both physical and spiritual consolation/nourishment to us. We see Jesus providing living waters for those weary and thirsty. For example, the Samaritan woman (Jn 4:4-42). She was thirsty for love and acceptance. People of her village gossiped about her; no one wanted to associate with her, and she felt ashamed to be seen in public. This is why she came to draw water from the well at a time when no one else would be there: It was about noon (the sixth hour). The sun would be overhead and it would be very hot, and no one else would come out to the well at that time. But the Lord Jesus made himself available to her at that time of the day, when she did not expect anyone there: "Jacob's well was there, and so Jesus, wearied as he was with his journey, sat down beside the well" (Jn 4:6).

The Samaritan woman came to draw water from that well. Jesus knew her real thirst and weariness. She was thirsty for God's mercy, acceptance, affection, and healing. Jesus provided all this for her by giving her the living waters of his word, and immediately she went to her village and began to witness to what Jesus had done in her life.

Before she met Jesus, she avoided meeting any person of the village, but after meeting Jesus, she went to those very people in her new role of witness to Jesus. "Many Samaritans from that city believed in Jesus because of the woman's testimony, 'He told me all that I ever did.' And many more believed because of his word" (Jn 4:39-41).

One beautiful and striking thing to note in the ministry of Jesus is that often he took time out to minister to individual persons in their particular need, and not only to crowds and groups. "He makes me lie down in green pastures, he restores my soul." We too can say confidently, "Jesus came for *me*."

Another example of Jesus giving rest and nourishment to the hungry people who came to listen to him is this:

> As Jesus went ashore, he saw a great crowd; and he had compassion for them . . . and he began to teach them many things . . . When it grew late, his disciples came to him and said, "send them away so that they may go and buy something for themselves to eat." But Jesus answered them, "You give them something to eat" . . . Taking the five loaves and the two fish, he looked up to heaven and blessed and broke the loaves, and gave them to his disciples to set before the people; and he divided the two fish among them all. And all ate and were filled (Mk 6:34-44).

Jesus restores our soul first of all with his word. His speaks his word and it melts our hearts, and so Jesus meets all our real needs.

This is what he did when crowds came to him; he "began to teach them many things."

I am reminded here of one of the words that Jesus spoke and which is a favorite of many people who need to be restored in their inner being, "Come to me, all you that are weary and are carrying heavy burdens, and I will give you rest" (Mt 11:28). The most wholesome rest can be found only in the loving presence and words of Jesus. Jesus is the good shepherd who knows the needs of his sheep. He leads us beside quiet waters and restores our soul, so that we can be strengthened to work with him and minister to others in need.

(3) "He leads me in the right paths, for his name's sake" (Ps 23:3b).

Jesus said, "Whoever follows me will never walk in darkness but will have the light of life . . . My sheep hear my voice. I know them, and they follow me . . . Whoever serves me must follow me" (Jn 8:12; 10:27; 12:26).

Jesus is the righteous and true Master who leads his disciples into the "right paths," and with him we can never go astray. A disciple's life shows the Master's goodness and wisdom. A disciple becomes discerning and holy by following faithfully in the footsteps of the Master. Jesus leads us in the direction that leads to the Father, the God of all life. And Jesus does this not because we deserve this attention, but because he is Jesus and "holy is his name" (Mt 6:9; Lk 1:49).

Moreover, Jesus expresses great trust in us. He says, "My sheep hear my voice. I know them, and they follow me." It is almost as if Jesus is boasting about his genuine disciples, he is proud of them. Are we worthy of such boasting? Left to ourselves, we are not at all worthy. But because we belong to Jesus and to his flock, we are made worthy by the Holy Spirit. Our dignity and worth comes from Jesus himself, and from being a member of the body of Christ, which is the Church. We form part of the flock that belongs to Jesus, the good Shepherd, who lays down his life for his flock. So too, St. Paul comforted himself by acknowledging that though he was far from perfect and had not yet reached the goal, nevertheless he could be absolutely confident that "Christ Jesus has made me his own" (see Phil 3:12-14).

Jesus says, "Whoever serves me must follow me." Following Jesus is an imperative for true disciples. To follow Jesus is not literally to walk behind him or slavishly imitate him, but to live our life as Jesus did. It means that we must have "the mind of Jesus."

Children learn first of all by imitating people closest to them. And Jesus calls us to "change and become like little children." One of the real ways in which we can become children is by starting to live as Jesus lived (in total dependence on the Father), to speak as Jesus would have us speak (always to build up rather than to destroy), to do whatever Jesus asks us to do (putting into practice Gospel-values and Gospel-relationships), and to receive all our joy in the knowledge that we belong to his family and that he will never forsake us.

Jesus is not like false teachers/leaders who, at the slightest inkling of danger to themselves, leave their followers and run away to save their own lives. Jesus said,

> The thief comes to steal and kill and destroy; I came that they may have life and have it abundantly. I am the good shepherd. The good shepherd lays down his life for the sheep (Jn 10:10-11).

The psalmist goes on to express deep trust in the Lord, the good shepherd, who carries his staff and rod that give security, protection, and hope to the sheep.

(4) "Even though I walk through the darkest valley, I fear no evil; for you are with me; your rod and your staff, they comfort me" (Ps 23:4).

First of all, I see Jesus himself praying these words, especially during his passion and suffering. The Sacred Scriptures that Jesus knew was the Old Testament, namely the Hebrew Scriptures. Hence he knew his Father God also as a Good Shepherd, who was always with him to comfort and strengthen him. The prophet Ezekiel speaks on behalf of God as the Good Shepherd, saying:

> *I myself will be the shepherd of my sheep, and I will make them lie down, says the Lord GOD . . . and I will bind up the injured and I will strengthen the weak . . .*
>
> *They shall know that I, the LORD their God, am with them . . . You are my sheep, the sheep of my pasture and I am your God, says the Lord GOD (Ezek 34:11-31).*

I believe that Jesus both prayed this psalm, and also perfectly fulfilled it in himself. Our own experience tells us this! We also recall St. Paul's experience of Jesus comforting and strengthening him with his rod and staff:

> *We are afflicted in every way, but not crushed; perplexed, but not driven to despair; persecuted, but not forsaken; struck down, but not destroyed; always carrying in the body the death of Jesus, so that the life of Jesus may also be manifested in our bodies (2 Cor 4:7-10).*

For St. Paul, Jesus' rod and staff was his cross, which gave Paul all the strength and comfort that he needed. To the Corinthians, who were tempted to bypass the cross of Christ to find glory only in the resurrection, he said, "For the word of the cross is folly to those who are perishing, but to us who are being saved it is the power of God" (1 Cor 1:18).

There are many people who are afraid of the "rod and the staff." They do not surrender their lives to the Good Shepherd. They follow lesser leaders anywhere just to feel secure and comfortable. In fact, they are afraid of being persecuted for the sake of the Master who is the good shepherd. St. Paul speaks of such people, saying,

> It is those who want to make a good showing that would compel you . . . only in order that they may not be persecuted for the cross of Christ . . . But far be it from me to glory except in the cross of our Lord Jesus Christ (Gal 6:12, 14).

Jesus never shirked the responsibilities given to him by the Father for our salvation, nor does he want us to be afraid in the moments of darkness and difficulty, for he is with us, his cross comforts us and gives us light. Therefore, we can sing out to Jesus,

> Surely goodness and kindness shall follow me all the days of my life; and I shall dwell in the house of the LORD for ever (Ps 23:6).

Amen.

PSALM 24

Lift up your heads, O gates!
And be lifted up, O ancient doors!
that the King of glory may come in.
Who is the King of glory?
The LORD, *strong and mighty,*
the LORD, *mighty in battle.*

Lift up your heads, O gates!
and be lifted up, O ancient doors!
that the King of glory may come in.
Who is this King of glory?
The LORD *of hosts, he is the King of glory (Ps 24:7-10).*

Jesus is the King of glory! He is the Lord for whom the gates of heaven were opened, and he is the Lord for whom the ancient doors of the temple were lifted up. When Jesus was an infant, he came to the temple for the first time. Mary and Joseph, his parents, "brought him up to Jerusalem to present him to the Lord" (Lk 2:22-25).

St. Luke tells us that even at this time of the presentation of Jesus in the temple, people recognized him as the Lord who is the King of glory. He describes an old man Simeon, filled with the Spirit of the Lord, a righteous and devout man, waiting to see the One who was to bring consolation and redemption to the people of Israel:

> *It had been revealed to him by the Holy Spirit that he should*
> *not see death before he had seen the Lord's Christ. And inspired*
> *by the Spirit, he came into the temple . . . took the child Jesus*
> *in his arms and blessed God and said, "Lord, now let your ser-*
> *vant depart in peace, according to your word; for my eyes have*
> *seen your salvation which you have prepared in the presence*

of all the people, a light for revelation to the Gentiles, and for glory to your people Israel."

And there was a prophetess, Anna . . . of a great age . . . She did not depart from the temple, worshipping with fasting and prayer night and day. And coming up at that very hour, she gave thanks to God, and spoke of him (Jesus) to all who were looking for the redemption of Jerusalem (Lk 2:25-38).

The Father revealed the truth and glory of Jesus, his Son, to the poor and the humble. It was they who waited for him with steadfast faith and the longing of hope, and who lived with single-hearted devotion for the Lord. The old man Simeon and the old woman Anna were such people, and God rewarded them with the presence of his Christ ("the anointed One"). Jesus is the Christ of God (Lk 9:20), the one anointed by the Spirit of God (cf. Lk 4:18).

Again, the gates of the temple opened up a second time for Jesus, the Christ, when his parents brought him up for the feast of the Passover when he was twelve years of age. Jesus' heart was drawn to the temple in such a way that though still a boy, he felt at home in the temple, and did not go back to Nazareth with his parents and relatives. He stayed behind in the temple courts.

After three days of seeking him, Mary and Joseph "found him in the temple, sitting among teachers, listening to them and asking them questions; and all who heard him were amazed at his understanding and his answers" (Lk 2:46-47). His words to his anxious mother were, "How is it that you sought me? Did you not know that I must be in my Father's house?" (Lk 2:49). Jesus' heart recognized his Father's house and he did not want to go away from there. This shows us Jesus' thirst for the word of God, and his keen knowledge and love of the word of God. Even the teachers of the law were amazed at his answers. The verses of Ps 24 were wonderfully fulfilled in this event. How happy the gates of the temple must have been to have the King of glory come in and stay within the courts of the temple, speaking the word of God! How happy the courts of the temple to have the voice of Jesus resounding within them!

Jerusalem and the temple were the places where Jesus spent his last days too. We are told that after he had formed his disciples and apostles, after he had ministered in Galilee with his teachings and his works, he resolved to go to Jerusalem. St. Luke tells us: "When the days drew near for him to be received up, he set his face to go to Jerusalem" (Lk 9:51).

The words, "set his face to go to Jerusalem," express Jesus' firm decision to go to Jerusalem. Jesus knew very well what awaited him there, he knew that Jerusalem had stoned and killed all those whom God had sent to her (cf. Mt 23:37). He warned his apostles about what awaited him in Jerusalem, about his suffering, death and resurrection. He took the twelve aside and said to them,

> Behold, we are going up to Jerusalem, and everything that is written of the Son of man by the prophets will be accomplished. For he will be delivered to the Gentiles, and will be mocked and shamefully treated and spit upon; they will scourge him and kill him, and on the third day he will rise. But they understood none of these things (Lk 18:31-34).

Jesus came to Jerusalem riding on a colt, accompanied by a whole multitude of the disciples who "began to rejoice and praise God with a loud voice for all the mighty works that they had seen, saying, 'Blessed is the King who comes in the name of the Lord! Peace in heaven and glory in the highest!'" (Lk 19:37-38).

Jesus, the King of glory, came to Zion riding on a donkey, humble and majestic at the same time, drawing praises and glory from the hearts of all who believed in him and hoped for his glory.

Once again, the temple of Jerusalem and its gates experienced the presence of the Lord of glory. Jesus loved the temple because it was his "Father's house." He spent a lot of time there. He taught there. He drove out the vendors and moneychangers from its courts saying, "It is written, 'My house shall be a house of prayer'; but you have made it a den of robbers" (Lk 19:45-46).

Every nook and corner, every thing in the temple vibrated in response to the presence of Jesus within its walls. It was not only the gates and the doors of the temple that responded to the coming of Jesus by opening up for him, but the curtain of the temple also responded to the Suffering Messiah who hung on the cross and was soon to die and give up his spirit to the Father, so that the Father and the Son together could send the Holy Spirit.

By dying on the cross, Jesus opened the way to the Father so that there was no need any more of a curtain to hide God's presence from the ordinary people of God. We read how when Jesus hung on the cross and it was about noon, "there was darkness over the whole land until three in the afternoon, while the sun's light failed; and the curtain of the temple was torn in two" (Lk 23:45).

God and humankind were reconciled once for all by the salvation that Jesus brought us through his death and resurrection. St. Paul says,

"While we were enemies, we were reconciled to God by the death of his Son ... we also rejoice in God through our Lord Jesus Christ, through whom we have now received our reconciliation" (Rom 5:10-11).

Thus, every time Jesus comes to us, this song of the psalmist can resound within the walls of our hearts and minds, so that we can open our doors to the Redeemer, for he comes with salvation and glory: "Lift up your heads, O gates! and be lifted up, O ancient doors! that the King of glory may come in."

PSALM 31

Into your hands I commit my spirit (Ps 31:5a).

We hear the words of this psalm on the lips of Jesus just before he died. They are the last words he cried out loudly, from the cross. Jesus is the Suffering Servant of God who, for our transgressions became obedient to the point of death on a cross.

> *It was now about noon, and darkness came over the whole land...Then Jesus, crying out with a loud voice, said, "Father, into your hands I commend my spirit." Having said this, he breathed his last (Lk 23:44-46).*

Jesus, the Innocent Sufferer, the Righteous One, entrusted his spirit to his God. This means that he abandoned himself totally into God's power, to be in union with the Father, as the Father's treasured possession. Jesus came from God and he returned to God, having completed the task of redemption for which he was sent. The world and all of humanity would never be the same again after the great saving work accomplished by Jesus Christ the Savior. Every human person has been redeemed by the blood of Jesus Christ, once and for all.

During his life on earth, Jesus remained in profound and full union with the heavenly Father. There was not a moment when he was not in union with God. With boundless love, Jesus accomplished our reconciliation with the Father; with full trust in his gracious Father, Jesus concluded his life of obedience to God's will here on earth. Jesus drank the cup of suffering to the full, the very same cup which he once dreaded while praying in the Garden of Gethsemane, saying: "Abba, Father, for you all things are possible; remove this cup from me; yet, not what I want, but what you want" (Mk 14:36).

God always wanted us to be saved. When God's first human creatures sinned against him, already then the Father promised a Savior who would crush the head of the vile serpent, the enemy of love and reconciliation (cf. Gen 3:15). Furthermore, through the prophet Isaiah, God made known this saving act of his in advance:

> *See my servant shall prosper; he shall be exalted and lifted up, and shall be very high. Just as there were many who were astonished at him, so marred was his appearance, beyond human semblance, and his form beyond that of mortals, so he shall startle many nations; kings shall shut their mouths because of him; for that which had not been told them they shall see, and that which they had not heard they shall contemplate (Is 52:13-15).*

Jesus always said and did only what would bring glory to the Father. He fulfilled all the promises of God. Nor was he deterred by the pain and suffering that he had to undergo to do God's will. As he neared his passion and death, Jesus manifested his intimate union with the Father. Jesus said,

> *Now my soul is troubled. And what should I say "Father, save me from this hour?" No, it is for this reason that I have come to this hour. Father, glorify your name. Then a voice came from heaven, "I have glorified it, and I will glorify it again." Jesus said, "This voice has come for your sake, not for mine ... And I, when I am lifted up from the earth, will draw all people to myself" (Jn 12:27-32).*

Therefore, on the cross, knowing that all things had been accomplished, Jesus entrusted his spirit to his Father, the God of the living. "Into thy hand I commit my spirit" (Ps 31:5a).

PSALM 40

Sacrifice and offering you do not desire, but you have given me an open ear. Burnt offering and sin offering you have not required. Then I said, "Here I am; in the scroll of the book it is written of me. I delight to do your will, O my God; your law is within my heart" (Ps 40:6-8).

As we continue to contemplate the face of Jesus more deeply, we notice more and more characteristics of our beloved Lord. Jesus always had "an open ear," as the psalmist says here. Jesus always listened to the voice of those who cried out to him. He even listened and responded to the cries that were not spoken out aloud. He had an open ear and an open heart and no one was, or is, excluded from his loving attention.

There is no other person that I can think of who, all through his life from childhood to adulthood, constantly delighted in the will of God more than Jesus, the beloved Son of God. Even when it cost him much trouble and shame, he rejoiced to do God's will. That was his sole purpose in life: to choose to do God's will, no matter what. Hence the words of this psalm can be seen to be wonderfully perfected in Jesus, "Here I am; in the scroll of the book it is written of me. I delight to do your will, O my God."

The letter to the Hebrews declares that these words of the psalm were perfectly fulfilled in the words and works of Jesus Christ, the Lamb of God. In the previous section, as we contemplated the face of Jesus in the books of the law (Pentateuch), we saw how the Jewish worshippers and priests offered burnt offerings and sin offerings year after year, using the blood of animals, such as goats and bulls. But the author of the letter to the Hebrews says,

In these sacrifices, there is a reminder of sin year after year. For it is impossible for the blood of bulls and goats to take away sins. Consequently, when Christ came into the world, he

said, "*Sacrifices and offerings you have not desired, but a body you have prepared for me; in burnt offerings and sin offerings you have taken no pleasure. Then I said, See, God, I have come to do your will, O God (in the scroll of the book it is written of me)."*

. . . He abolishes the first (law) in order to establish the second (God's will). And it is by God's will that we have been sanctified through the offering of the body of Jesus Christ once for all (Heb 10:4-10).

The letter further explains that the sacrifices that every priest offered year after year could never take away sins. But when Jesus Christ had offered for all time a single sacrifice for sins, "he sat down at the right hand of God. For by a single sacrifice he has perfected for all time those who are sanctified. And the Holy Spirit also testifies to us . . . Where there is forgiveness of these (sins), there is no longer any offering for sin" (Heb 10:11-18).

Thus, in the fullness of time, "God sent his Son, born of a woman, born under the law, to redeem those who were under the law" (Gal 4:4). Jesus redeemed all humanity and creation once for all. This is why we can say with St. Paul today that,

Neither death, nor life, nor angels, nor rulers, nor things present, nor things to come, now powers, nor height, nor depth, nor anything else (including sin) in all of creation will be able to separate us from the love of God in Christ Jesus our Lord (Rom 8:38-39).

PSALM 46

God is our refuge and strength, a very present help in trouble. There-
fore we will not fear, though the earth should change, though the
mountains shake in the heart of the sea; though its waters roar and
foam, though the mountains tremble with its tumult . . . The LORD of
hosts is with us (Ps 46:1-3, 7).

How wonderfully Jesus shines forth in these words of the psalm!
Let us recall the evening when Jesus was quite tired and needed
to rest awhile and sleep, as Mark tells us. All day Jesus had been
teaching the crowds about the Kingdom of God in parables, and
working wonders in their lives even as they listened to him. In the
evening he said to the disciples,

> *Let us go across to the other side. And leaving the crowd, they*
> *took him with them, just as he was, in the boat (Mk 4:35, 36).*

The words, "just as he was," seem to say something about the
physical condition of Jesus at the end of a very tiring day. He often
taught the crowds from the boat. Perhaps in this case too he sat in
his disciples' boat and taught the crowds from there. The whole day
had gone by, and Jesus still continued to minister with word and
action to the yearning crowds. As evening came, we can imagine
Jesus in need of quiet and rest. He asked his disciples to sail the
boat to the other side of the large lake. As soon as they set sail, Jesus
put his head down on a cushion and immediately fell fast asleep.

> *And a great storm of wind arose, and the waves beat into the*
> *boat, so that the boat was already filling. But he was in the*
> *stern, asleep on the cushion; and they woke him and said to*
> *him, "Teacher, do you not care if we perish?" (Mk 4:37, 38).*

Here we see once again the evil tactics of the enemy. He grabbed
this moment to his advantage when Jesus was much in need of rest

and in fact was fast asleep. First, the enemy did not want Jesus to get any rest, so that all his energy would wane and he would not be able to work the great wonder that he was going to do on the other side of the lake (Mk 5:1-20). Second, he played on the mind of the disciples too by instigating great fear and panic into them, a fear of the terrible storm and panic because of the possibility of drowning. It is a striking paradox to notice that these men were skilled fishermen, and this certainly was not the first time that they were experiencing a storm in the sea. Yet, they were frantic with fear. Here is a good example for us to recognize that where fear is strong, faith becomes very weak. Jesus pointed out this truth to the disciples.

> And (Jesus) awoke and rebuked the wind, and said to the sea, "Peace! Be still!" And the wind ceased, and there was a great calm. He said to them, "Why are you afraid? Have you no faith?" And they were filled with awe, and said to one another, "Who then is this, that even wind and sea obey him?" (Mk 4:39-41).

Those in the boat with Jesus then arrived at a point of their relationship with Jesus where they were in awe of him. They saw his glory, they experienced his power, they accepted his Lordship over all of creation.

When such is the experience of any disciple of Jesus, then the only response is silence, a worshipping silence, a surrendering of the heart and soul to God who says in this psalm,

> Be still, and know that I am God! I am exalted among the nations, I am exalted in the earth (Ps 46:10).

When God reveals his dynamic glory and majesty, he invites us to wait on him and recognize his work, knowing that he alone is God who can do all things. In response, we can express our faith in him and allow him to work in our lives, as Mary did when the angel Gabriel told her, "with God nothing will be impossible" (Lk 1:37).

The disciples experienced this divine presence of Jesus in another boat-incident, when again they were drawn to worship Jesus the Lord "exalted in the earth." After the great multiplication of loaves and fish, St. Mark tells us that Jesus took leave of the disciples and the crowd and "went into the hills to pray" (Mk 6:46).

And when evening came, the boat was out on the sea, and he was alone on the land. And he saw that they were distressing in rowing, for the wind was against them. And about the fourth watch of the night he came to them, walking on the sea. He meant to pass by them, but when they saw him walking on the sea they thought it was a ghost, and cried out; they all saw him and were terrified. But immediately he spoke to them and said, "Take heart, it is I; have no fear." And he got into the boat with them and the wind ceased. And they were utterly astounded (Mk 6:47-51).

Once again, the skilled, grown-up fishermen cry out with fear, they are terrified because they think they are seeing a ghost. (Not only some amongst us today are afraid of ghosts, even the disciples had the same fear!) Of course, Jesus heals them, he delivers them out of that fear. Jesus tells them that even the sea is under his Lordship and power, he is the Lord exalted on the sea and the land. And when Jesus is with us, what is there to fear? Hence, one good way of getting rid of our fears of darkness, etc., is to remain constantly with Jesus through mental prayer and faith in his words. For Jesus says, "Fear not, it is I" who am with you.

We can also take words of Psalm 77:19 and add them here. The psalmist sings, "Your way was through the sea, your path, through the mighty waters; yet your footprints were unseen."

How true of Jesus, who came walking on the waters and manifesting his glory before his unbelieving disciples.

So come, let us worship our God who is "exalted among the nations and exalted in the earth" in the Person of Jesus Christ our Lord.

PSALM 50

Jesus followed and taught that true religion is a matter of the heart and involves a sincere relationship with God who is loving Father. It is a matter also of living out in everyday life what one believes in the heart and prays with the mouth.

But we have still not grasped the depth of Jesus' words and actions even today, for don't we continue to give preference to our desires over the demands of the Gospel? In ancient times, the chosen people of God behaved the same way too, even after God had made a covenant of love with them and was very close to them. Moses had pointed this out, saying, "What great nation is there that has a god so near to it as the LORD our God is to us, whenever we call upon him?" (Deut 4:7).

The People had readily responded to God saying, "Yes LORD, all that you have said we will do" (cf. Ex 19:8), but in practice they did not really heed God's voice nor walk in his ways. They found ways and means of living a comfortable worldly life, which was unchallenging and easygoing, and in conformity to this world's values. For this reason God spoke these words through the psalmist:

> What right have you to recite my statutes, or take my covenant on your lips? For you hate discipline, and you cast my words behind you. If you see a thief, you are a friend of his; and you keep company with adulterers. You give your mouth free rein for evil, and your tongue frames deceit. You sit and speak against your brother; you slander your own mother's son. These things you have done and I have been silent; you thought that I was one like yourself. But now I rebuke you, and lay the charge before you (Ps 50:16-21).

While reflecting on these words we can also recall a particular action of Jesus which echoed the tone and sentiments of these words of the psalm. We read that Jesus:

entered the temple and began to drive out those who sold and those who bought in the temple, and he over-turned the tables of the money-changers and the seats of those who sold pigeons; and he would not allow any one to carry anything through the temple. And he taught, and said to them, "Is it not written, My house shall be called a house of prayer for all the nations? But you have made it a den of robbers" (Mk 11:15-17).

Living a life that is conformed and accommodated to this world and its ideologies means making a mockery of our identity as members of the body of Christ, the Church. The Church is our home while we journey together to our Father's house. And "we cannot serve both God and mammon" at the same time (Lk 16:13).

On the other hand, there are those of us who have believed in God and in Jesus Christ, and have received many spiritual gifts. But the problem comes when we rely on the gifts of God as our ticket to heaven.

Just because we have certain spiritual gifts or charisms, such as that of prophecy, healing, casting out demons, etc., it does not mean that we have automatically become holy. In fact, we may well have become complacent with our inner lives, and started believing foolishly that we deserve or have earned these gifts from God, and that therefore our heavenly future is assured. With such complacency come also selfishness and pride, and soon we can be caught unawares and fall into the enemy's trap. He attacks where and when we are weakest. In moments of temptation we will not be able to overcome if our day-to-day lives are not in keeping with our faith in Jesus Christ and his life-giving words. Our lives must be built on the firm foundation of the word of God, or else we will be taken aback when our lives on earth come to an end. To save us from such peril to our eternal happiness, Jesus warns us,

Not every one who says to me, "Lord, Lord," shall enter the kingdom of heaven, but he who does the will of my Father who

is in heaven. On that day many will say to me, "Lord, Lord, did we not prophesy in your name, and cast out demons in your name, and do many mighty works in your name?" And then will I declare to them, "I never knew you; depart from me, you evildoers" (Mt 7:21-23).

Let us seek the Lord and his righteousness, and all else will be given to us. For Jesus is drawn to the person who has a contrite and humble heart, and takes his words seriously.

PSALM 51

This is one of the most beautiful and touching prayers of repentance that we can use for ourselves. In fact, the Church prays it every Friday morning in the liturgy of the hours. David prayed this psalm when he realized, with the help of the Holy Spirit, how foolish and weak he was, and how his heart and its passions had deceived him into sinning so grievously against God and his neighbor (cf. 2 Sam 11-12). David understood that being a king was no guarantee that he was also wise according to the Spirit's standards. He accepted that real power and goodness lie within one's heart, and that for this to develop one had to be wise and true in the inner being. Hence he prayed: "You desire truth in the inward being; therefore teach me wisdom in my secret heart" (Ps 51:6).

Jesus, the wisest of all sages and holiest of all holy people, knew how important it was to be wise and gentle in the "secret heart," a place known to God and the individual person alone. Hence, Jesus taught his disciples what was the proper manner in which to communicate with God:

> *Whenever you pray, go into your room and shut the door and pray to your Father who is in secret; and your Father who sees in secret will reward you (Mt 6:6).*

The Father "is in secret," the Father "sees in secret." Whatever one may appear to be in front of others, it is possible that this is all just show and lip service, if one's secret heart is not also attuned to one's outward actions. God sees the heart first. Hence, my secrets are no secrets to the Father. We may think, as David perhaps did, that whatever we do or say in secret would be hidden even from God. But the fact is that the Father knows all my thoughts and intentions even before I know them myself.

O LORD, you have searched me and known me. You know when I sit down and when I rise up; you discern my thoughts from far away . . . Even before a word is on my tongue, O LORD, you know it completely (Ps 139:1-4).

Recognizing this profound truth, let us also desire truth in the inner being and wisdom of heart. Wisdom is a gift of the Spirit to all who desire and long for it. One way of obtaining this gift is to become truly God-fearing, that is, to give God and his holy will first place in our lives, and to relate with God as a child with the loving Father.

The sages, in all the Books of Wisdom in the Bible, have said, "The fear of the Lord is the beginning of wisdom." They speak of a loving reverential fear that rejects all evil and selfishness, in order to remain united with the Lord in one's heart and mind and actions. This "fear of the Lord" is also a messianic gift of the Spirit (Is 11:1ff) to those who long and ask for it. The psalmist prays further, "Create in me a clean heart, O God, and put a new and right spirit within me" (Ps 51:10).

Jesus taught in the Beatitudes, "Blessed are the pure in heart, for they shall see God" (Mt 5:8). It is those who have a pure heart who can recognize God working in their lives day after day. Purity of heart brings the greater gift of constant companionship with God. All the saints obtained this, both as a gift from God and also from their efforts to remain united with God every moment of their lives. They suffered much, they were tempted much, they faced many trials, but they never gave in to feelings of hatred and revenge, or self-pity and discouragement.

We are called today by Jesus to have a pure heart, the promise is that we will be among those blessed with a constant awareness of the presence of God in and around us, wherever we may be and in all circumstances of our lives. Moreover, our hearts will become strong and courageous, full of love for God and neighbor. And the Holy Spirit will dwell in us and be our Counselor and Friend.

With the Spirit in our hearts we will sing out the praises of God our Father and of the Lord Jesus Christ.

The psalmist asks God to touch and open his lips so that they can declare the praises of God before all peoples: "O LORD, open my lips, and my mouth will declare your praise" (Ps 51:15).

Praise of God is a wonderful form of prayer that we can practice every day. When we praise God, our attention is on him and his wonderful glory. Jesus too praised the Father all the time. He taught us how to pray to God who is Father, and the prayer begins with praise of God: "Our Father in heaven, hallowed be your name" (Mt 6:9).

God is to be praised for he is not far away from us, he is our Father and not a stranger or someone who is only interested in punishing us. Rather, he is the one whose arms are open wide with love and mercy for us, for he is our Father in Jesus Christ our Redeemer. God is to be praised for his name is holy, and he makes us holy by his word of truth and by his Spirit.

Jesus praised and thanked the Father because his ways are holy and wonderful, his thoughts far beyond our thoughts. God reveals himself to the humble and small people whom the world thinks nothing of, but God makes his deeds known among them so that they can boast of the Lord and not of themselves. God rejoices and celebrates when a sinner returns to him with a humble and contrite heart, just as David did in this psalm. For and with all such people, Jesus praises God saying,

> I thank you, Father, Lord of heaven and earth, because you have hidden these things from the wise and intelligent and have revealed them to infants; yes, Father, for such was your gracious will (Mt 11:25).

The gracious will of God is to seek and save the lost through Jesus our Savior (cf. Lk 19:10). If we hear the Lord's voice today, let us return to him and receive his Spirit so that we can become his witnesses to all who are yet to meet Jesus in their lives.

Restore to me the joy of your salvation, and sustain in me a willing spirit. Then I will teach transgressors your ways, and sinners will return to you (Ps 51:12-13).

PSALM 55

But it is you my companion, my familiar friend, with whom I kept company ... My companion laid hands on a friend and violated a covenant with me with speech smoother than butter, but with a heart set on war; with words that were softer than oil, but in fact were drawn swords (Ps 55:13-14, 20-21).

These prophetic words of the psalmist bring to our mind the treacherous "friendship" of Judas with Jesus. After a whole night in prayer, Jesus had chosen his twelve apostles, among whom was Judas Iscariot (cf. Lk 6:12-16). The twelve were to be the closest friends of Jesus. In fact, they were his core team, and Jesus trained them with great care and skill.

Yet, Jesus never forced his will on any one of them. He gave them full freedom to follow him, or to go away. His teaching always was, "If you love me, you will keep my commandments" (Jn 14:15). Many disciples did stop following Jesus and they went away, because following him and obeying his teachings was too difficult for them (cf. Jn 6:60-66).

But Judas did not go away from Jesus or leave him sooner, as some others did. He stayed with Jesus, yet his mind did not fully consent to Jesus and all that Jesus stood for. On the quiet, he joined hands with those religious leaders who wanted to kill Jesus. Judas perhaps thought that thereby he was doing his religious duty, and he accepted payment for his betrayal of Jesus. His mind was so tightly closed that when he did begin to feel remorse, he did not do it fully; he preferred to end his life by his own hands, rather than turn to Jesus in full repentance.

Being one of the twelve apostles who always knew where Jesus would be during the day or the night, he got a chance to have Jesus arrested in the Garden of Gethsemane. Just a few moments before this, Jesus had been praying with much anguish to the Father, and had accepted to let the Father's will be done to its completion. Then Judas arrived. We read:

*Judas, one of the twelve, was leading them. He approached
Jesus to kiss him; but Jesus said to him, "Judas, is it with a kiss
that you are betraying the Son of Man?" Jesus said to the chief
priests, the officers of the temple police, and the elders who had
come for him, "Have you come out with swords and clubs as
if I were a bandit? When I was day after day in the temple, you
did not lay hands on me. But this is your hour, and the power
of darkness!" (Lk 22:47-53).*

Yes, it was indeed darkness that had entered Judas' heart so that
he totally turned away from Jesus. We read in the account of the
Last Supper in the fourth Gospel that Jesus, being troubled in
spirit, testified,

*Truly, truly, I say to you, one of you will betray me . . . When
Jesus had dipped the morsel, he gave it to Judas, the son of
Simon Iscariot. Then after the morsel, Satan entered into
him . . . after receiving the morsel, he immediately went out;
and it was night (Jn 13:21-30).*

The treacherous betrayal by Judas had been prophetically
remarked upon by the psalmist centuries earlier in Ps 41:9: "Even
my bosom friend in whom I trusted, who ate of my bread, has lifted
the heel against me."

Jesus quoted these words of the psalm when he told his disciples, "I am not speaking of all of you; I know whom I have chosen. But it is to fulfill the scripture, 'The one who ate my bread has
lifted his heel against me.' I tell you this now, before it occurs, so
that when it occurs, you may believe that I am he" (Jn 13:18-19).

All that Jesus suffered at the hands of his beloved and closest
disciples, especially Judas Iscariot, God turned for our good and
the salvation of the whole world. Jesus transformed darkness into
light, and treachery into love. Jesus became our reconciliation
with God (cf. Rom 5:11).

Hence, today we have so much more a reason to cling to Jesus and obey his word, for in so doing Jesus will be our victory and consolation in the storms and seductions of our life in this passing world.

PSALM 69

For my thirst, they gave me vinegar to drink (Ps 69:21b).

What happened many centuries after this psalm was written, is well known to us all:

> *Jesus, knowing that all was now finished, said, "I thirst." A bowl full of vinegar stood there; so they put a sponge full of the vinegar on hyssop and held it to his mouth (Jn 19:28-29).*

Even if a thirsty enemy says, "I am thirsty, please give me something to drink," we would unhesitatingly give water to the one who thirsts. But when Jesus felt thirsty, after all the liquid in his body was drained through his bleeding and sweating and wounds, the soldiers gave him a sponge soaked in *vinegar* to drink! Since the previous day's Last Supper, Jesus had not had anything to drink. More than twelve hours of physical torture had followed, and now in a very dehydrated condition, Jesus was thirsty. But all they gave him was vinegar. Such was the extent of inhumanity that Jesus experienced from his persecutors.

I would like to reflect on Jesus' thirst in the spiritual sense also. Jesus' thirst is a thirst for God, as the psalmist put it, "O God my God, my soul thirsts for you; my flesh faints for you, like a dry weary land without water" (Ps 63:1).

As we saw in an earlier psalm, Jesus experienced the deep agony of the silence of God, and he cried out, "My God, my God, why have you forsaken me?" (Ps 22:1). In this agonizing hour, when Jesus suffered all this because of the sins of all humanity, Jesus continued to focus his attention on God. He thirsted to do the will of the Father to the very end. It is as if he was saying to God, "I thirst for your will to be fully accomplished through me, my Father." Jesus was committed to doing God's will fully *on our behalf*, even if a terrible and shameful death on the cross was to be the end result.

> *O the depth of the riches and wisdom and knowledge of God!*
> *How unsearchable are his judgments and how inscrutable his*
> *ways! (Rom 11:33).*

Faced with such a mystery of divine love and fidelity, salvation and righteousness, power and victory, we can only bow our knees and worship our Lord Jesus Christ, to him be glory for ever. Amen.

PSALM 89 and 132

(1) *You have said, "I have made a covenant with my chosen one, I have sworn to my servant David: I will establish your descendants forever; I have set the crown on one who is mighty, I have exalted one chosen from the people . . . With my holy oil I have anointed him . . . My faithfulness and steadfast love shall be with him"* (Ps 89:3-4, 19-24).

He shall cry to me, "You are my Father, my God" . . . I will establish his line forever, and his throne as long as the heavens endure (Ps 89:26, 29).

The psalmist addresses his words to God the Almighty Father. And in turn the psalmist hears God declaring that He has made a covenant with the chosen and anointed servant-king David, from whose line will come the chosen one, on whom God will set the everlasting crown. This descendant will be very beloved and will have an intimate personal relationship with God as his Father.

These words contain a true picture of Jesus, the Son of God, who was anointed by the Holy Spirit from the moment of his conception in Mary's womb, and who established God's kingdom on earth in a way that will never end.

The angel said to Mary,

Do not be afraid, Mary, for you have found favor with God. And now, you will conceive in your womb and bear a son, and you will name him Jesus. He will be great, and will be called the Son of the Most High, and the Lord God will give to him the throne of his ancestor David. He will reign over the house of Jacob forever, and of his kingdom there will be no end (Lk 1:30-33).

In Psalm 132 also, we read words that echo the same sentiments of Ps 89. The psalmist says,

The LORD swore to David ... "One of your sons I will set on your throne." For the LORD has chosen Zion; he has desired it for his habitation ... "There I will make a horn to sprout for David; I have prepared a lamp for my anointed. His enemies I will clothe with shame, but upon himself, his crown will shed its luster" (Ps 132:11-18).

One can see that the historical person spoken about here is Jesus, the son of David about whom the psalm sings. The psalmist also speaks of the chosen place for the Messiah's habitation, namely Zion or Jerusalem. In Jesus' case, the "habitation" referred to is not his hometown Nazareth, but Jerusalem, where the Father would triumph in his Son.

We have seen how Jesus loved Jerusalem from his first known personal experience of it at the age of twelve (cf. Ps 24 above). When Jesus began his public ministry after his baptism in the Jordan, he knew that the city would be the place where he would be killed, just like all the prophets before him (cf. Lk 13:34-35; 19:41-44). Jesus' experiences of the passion, death and glorious resurrection were all in the city of Jerusalem. It was again in Jerusalem that the Spirit was poured out in a mighty and manifest way on Pentecost day (Acts 2), and from Jerusalem the word went forth and was preached to the ends of the earth (cf. Acts 1:8).

(2) *"I will make him the firstborn, the highest of the kings of the earth" (Ps 89:27).*

Jesus is this firstborn. He is the pre-eminent one. He is the Alpha and the Omega. St. Paul describes this beautifully:

He is the image of the invisible God, the firstborn of all creation; for in him all things in heaven and on earth were created ... He himself is before all things, and in him all things hold together. He is the head of the body, the Church; he is the

*beginning, the firstborn from the dead, so that he might come
to have first place in everything (Col 1:15-18).*

Jesus is the Lord of all creation, for in him all things were created and in him the entire universe holds together. Thus, he is "the
firstborn of all creation." Jesus is also the first to experience the glorious resurrection from the dead, he is "the firstborn from the
dead." Because of him and in him, all of us have the hope of a resurrection from the dead.

St. Paul says in another letter, "Those whom (God) foreknew
he also predestined to be conformed to the image of his Son, in
order that he might be the firstborn within a large family" (Rom
8:29).

This refers to Jesus as the firstborn who founded the Church
(Family/Community of believers). This is the community of the
adopted children of God. We are the members of this family of God
whose "firstborn" (i.e. founder) is Jesus himself. This is why Jesus
is called, "the head of the body, the church" (Col 1:18). It follows
that we share the same vocation of giving our lives for others as
Jesus did. He is our Brother whose footsteps we are to follow till
we come to eternal life. Jesus teaches us to love and to forgive, to
follow the ways that lead to life and fruitfulness for the sake of the
kingdom of God. In this walk we are not alone, for he has told us,
"I am with you always, to the end of the age" (Mt 28:20).

PSALM 107

(1) *Some were sick through their sinful ways ... Then they cried to the* L*ORD* *in their trouble and he saved them ... he sent out his word and healed them (Ps 107:17-20).*

He sent out his word and healed them." We read in the Gospel narratives about four friends of a paralyzed man who open up the roof of a house in order to lower their friend on a mat in front of Jesus for healing. Jesus' first words are: "Son, your sins are forgiven you." And later he says, "Stand up, take up your mat and go home" (Mk 2:5-11).

Another time, when Jesus met a man who had been paralyzed for thirty-eight years and who lay by the pool of five porticoes, Jesus said, "'Do you want to be made well? ... Stand up, take your mat and walk' ... Later Jesus found him in the temple and said to him, 'See you have been made well! Do not sin any more, so that nothing worse happens to you'" (Jn 5:6b-9, 14).

Yet another time, a centurion implored Jesus to heal his servant. Jesus wanted to go to his house and heal him. But the centurion, who had immense faith in the command of Jesus, said, "Lord, I am not worthy to have you come under my roof; but only speak the word, and my servant will be healed ... And Jesus said, 'Go; let it be done for you according to your faith.' And the servant was healed in that hour" (Mk 8:5-13).

(2) *Some went down to the sea doing business on the mighty waters ... the stormy wind lifted up the waves to heaven ... their courage melted away ... they reeled and staggered like drunkards, and were at wits' end. Then they cried to the* L*ORD* *in their trouble and ... he made the storm be still, and the waves of the sea were hushed (Ps 107:23-30).*

These verses of the psalm remind us of the incident when Jesus was asleep in a boat and,

> *a windstorm arose on the sea, so great that the boat was being swamped by the waves. The disciples woke him up saying, "Lord, save us! We are perishing!" And he got up and rebuked the winds and the sea; and there was a dead calm (Mt 8:23-27).*

Jesus, the Son of God and the Son of Mary, is the fulfillment of all the prayers and longing of the psalmists. Jesus prayed the psalms all his life, and then fulfilled their prophecies in his words and works.

PSALM 118

The stone that the builders rejected has become the chief cornerstone.
This is the LORD's doing; it is marvelous in our eyes (Ps 118:22-23).

The three Synoptic Gospels of Matthew, Mark, and Luke have all
quoted this text from the psalms in its proper context. They have
done so in the parable of the "wicked tenants" (cf. Mt 21:42; Mk
12:10; Lk 20:17). Jesus taught this parable in the temple, in the
presence of the elders and chief priests and scribes who were jealous of him, and were always seeking to find fault with him and also
do away with him.

In the parable Jesus speaks about the tenants who refused to
give the required share of the produce of the vineyard to the master who had sent his servants to collect it. The master sent servant
after servant, but the tenants on the vineyard seized and beat one
and killed another and stoned another. Finally, the master sent his
own son to them, thinking that they would heed him, but the tenants dealt even more treacherously with the son. "They seized
him, threw him out of the vineyard, and killed him" (Mt 21:39).

Then Jesus asked, "What then will the owner of the vineyard
do to them? He will come and destroy those tenants and give the
vineyard to others." When they heard this, they said, "Heaven for-
bid!" But he looked at them and said, "What then does this text
mean: 'The stone that the builders rejected has become the cornerstone?'" (Lk 20:17).

The evangelists tell us, "When the scribes and chief priests realized that he had told this parable against them, they wanted to lay
hands on him at that very hour" (Lk 20:19; Mk 12:12; Mt 21:45).

This exposes the falsehood, hard heartedness, and craftiness of
the chief priests and the scribes. They understood that they were
the builders, they were the "wicked tenants" of the parable. They
had not been faithful ministers of the word to the people, they had
not obeyed the word themselves. For if they had believed and

accepted God's word, they would not have killed the true prophets whom God sent to them (Lk 13:34).

Once again the word of God through Jesus was inviting them to change and become true builders, chosen by God. However, though they should have recognized that Jesus was truly sent by God, they did not do so. What is more evil is that they wanted to kill him, as their ancestors had done to the prophets in the past. Hence, Jesus is the "stone rejected by the builders," but which has "become the cornerstone."

Every stone cannot be a cornerstone. The cornerstone is a keystone or a capstone that can fit into the center and make a perfect arch. It alone can hold up a building by its fitting into the corner of the wall where another ordinary stone cannot fit, without being broken or chipped to size. A cornerstone is also quite sharp because it had a conical edge. Hence the words, "Everyone who falls on the stone will be broken to pieces; and it will crush anyone on whom it falls" (Lk 20:18). Spiritually, this refers to the purification and change that one experiences when one believes and opens one's heart to Jesus.

It is truly generous of Jesus that he does not personally condemn the scribes and the chief priests. He tells the parable to give them another opportunity to come to their senses and repent of their hard heartedness and pride, and heed the voice of God. In his blunt words there is much gentleness and hidden concern. Jesus wants to explain also, as the psalm says, "This is the Lord's doing; it is marvelous in our eyes" (also in Mt 21:42b, Mk 12:11).

The Lord's own doing has transformed the rejection of the keystone by the builders and made it a marvelous thing! St. Peter, speaking to the rulers, elders, scribes, and chief priests in the hearing of the council after the lame man was healed, explained,

> Let it be known to all of you, and to all the people of Israel, that this man is standing before you in good health by the name of Jesus Christ of Nazareth, whom you crucified, whom God raised from the dead. This Jesus is "the stone that was

rejected by you, the builders; it has become the cornerstone" (Acts 4:10-11).

The resurrection of Jesus from the dead is the marvelous thing that the Father has done. St. Peter speaks about the value of this whole marvel for our daily lives. He writes,

Come to him, a living stone, though rejected by mortals yet chosen and precious in God's sight, and like living stones, let yourselves be built into a spiritual house, to be a holy priest-hood, to offer spiritual sacrifices acceptable to God through Jesus Christ. For it stands in scripture: "Behold, I am laying in Zion a stone, a cornerstone chosen and precious, and he who believes in him will not be put to shame." To you therefore who believe, he is precious, but for those who do not believe, "The very stone which the builders rejected has become the head of the corner," and "A stone that will make men stumble, a rock that makes them fall"; for they stumble because they disobey the word . . . But you are a chosen race, a royal priesthood, a holy nation, God's own people, that you may proclaim the wonderful deeds of him who called you out of darkness into his marvelous light (1 Pt 2:4-9).

Let us, therefore, bless the Lord our God for the marvelous works he has worked for our salvation in Jesus Christ. Through the power of the Spirit he empowers and equips us to live our lives in this marvelous light of Jesus, and to lead others to this light that dispels all darkness.

"Blessed is the one who comes in the name of the LORD!" (Ps 118:26a). Jesus is the one who comes in the name of the Lord, bringing peace and harmony, healing and happiness, to a world wrought by selfishness, hatred and darkness. All who believe in him experience this wonder of Jesus in their lives, even in the midst of difficult trials and sorrows. Blessed be the name of the Lord!

PSALM 119

This beautiful psalm is the longest one in the book of Psalms, and it is a profound reflection on the value of the *word of God* in the believer's life. Every line of every verse speaks about the word in one form or another. Some of the alternatives that are used for the "word" are: "law," "ways," "precepts," "decrees," "commandments," "ordinances," "statutes," "promises," and "judgments."

Let us recall just a few incidents of Jesus' life in the context of this rich psalm.

> **(1)** *Though the cords of the wicked ensnare me, I do not forget thy law . . . The wicked lie in wait to destroy me, but I consider thy testimonies (Ps 119:61, 95).*

This was Jesus' experience during the temptations in the desert and during the trials after his arrest. However severely the enemy tried to trap Jesus, Jesus remembered the word of God and held it firmly as his weapon and strength against all the snares of the enemy. His accusers in the council accused him falsely, but Jesus did not seek his own will. Jesus knew why he was to die, and he carried the cross to Calvary because he is the Good Shepherd who lays down his life for his sheep. His sheep are all who believe in him.

> **(2)** *The arrogant smear me with lies, but with my whole heart I keep your precepts/words (Ps 119:69).*

As in the desert temptations, so also in his whole life and ministry, Jesus recognized that the devil was "the father of lies" (Jn 8:44) who was at work among unbelievers and believers, to keep the unbelievers from believing in the truth of Jesus, and to make the believers in Jesus doubt and fall away.

St. John tells us what Jesus said to the Jews:

Why do you not understand what I say? It is because you cannot accept my word. You are from your father the devil, and you choose to do your father's desires. He was a murderer from the beginning and does not stand in the truth, because there is no truth in him. When he lies, he speaks according to his nature, for he is a liar and the father of lies . . . Whoever is from God hears the words of God (Jn 8:43-47).

Jesus kept the light of the word of God within him, and allowed the word to lead and guide him at every step. We can easily imagine the constant prayer breathed by Jesus: "Your word is a lamp to my feet and a light to my path" (Ps 119:105).

(3) *I hold back my feet from every evil way, in order to keep your word (Ps 119:101).*

The letter to the Hebrews tell us that, "We do not have a high priest who is unable to sympathize with our weaknesses, but we have one who in every respect has been tempted as we are, yet without sin" (Heb 4:15).

Jesus is the faithful one who kept the word of truth in his life at all times, and thus overcame every temptation. It must have been difficult for him because he was fully human like us, but he had a pure heart willing to obey God's will and not follow his own desires. Let us learn from Jesus, as he himself says to us, "Learn from me, for I am gentle and humble in heart" (Mt 11:29).

"The sum of your word is truth" (Ps 119:160). Jesus prays to the Father for us, "Sanctify them in the truth; your word is truth" (Jn 17:17).

May we relish this beautiful psalm as we take some time to read it quietly and slowly and reflect on its value in our own lives. May we love the word of God and discover the meaning of our lives in the light of the word!

PSALM 139

For thou didst form my inward parts, thou didst knit me together in my mother's womb. I praise thee, for thou art fearful and wonderful. Wonderful are thy works! Thou knowest me right well; my frame was not hidden from thee, when I was being made in secret, intricately wrought in the depths of the earth. Thy eyes beheld my unformed substance (Ps 139:13-16).

Jesus was conceived in the womb of Mother Mary by the will of the Father and the work of the Holy Spirit. Indeed, when he was being intricately woven in the depths of Mary's womb, only God the Father knew his frame, for he knit together the baby Jesus in his mother's womb. These words of the psalm is every child's, every person's prayer of gratitude and wonder, but more than any one else, it was surely Jesus' song of childlike wonder and thanksgiving to the Father.

Mary must have been in awesome wonder and happiness every day with the experience of the baby growing in her womb. He must have had such a profound effect on her, every day of her pregnancy. Whenever she reflected on what his facial features might be, she must have been filled with joy to realize that his face would resemble her own, for she was his human mother and her womb was the place where Jesus developed his bodily shape, features and color! "Wonderful are thy works! Thou knowest me right well."

The face of Jesus was the face that the entire world was longing to see. Jesus' holy and radiant face was going to bring light to the world and to the lives of all who had longed for him. His face would bring joy and gladness to Mary and Joseph, to the shepherds and the wise men, to the angels and the poor. Jesus, Son of Mary, the Son of God, our Savior, come! Let us see your face, and be filled with joy!

When Christ came into the world, he said, "Sacrifices and offer-
ings thou hast not desired, but a body hast thou prepared for
me . . . Lo, I have come to do thy will, O God" (Heb 10:5-7).

The body that God the Father had prepared for Jesus his Son
came from the body of the Virgin of Nazareth, holy and chaste,
innocent and humble who, along with all the women of Israel, had
longed for the coming of the Messiah, the anointed one, the Savior. Mary was "full of grace" and had "found favor with God." She
was the faithful virgin whose only love was to do the will of her
God. This virtue of obedience was clearly shared with her son
Jesus, whose food was to do the will of the Father, as he told the
disciples, saying:

My food is to do the will of him who sent me, and to accom-
plish his work (Jn 4:34).

PSALM 150

Praise the LORD!
Praise God in his sanctuary; praise him in his mighty firmament!
Praise him for his mighty deeds; praise him according to his
  exceeding greatness!

Praise him with trumpet sound; praise him with lute and harp!
Praise him with timbrel and dance; praise him with strings and
  pipe!
Praise him with sounding cymbals; praise him with loud clashing
  cymbals!
Let everything that breathes praise the LORD!
Praise the LORD!

Why all this concert of praise? Among other reasons we can think, it is because THE LORD HAS RISEN INDEED! He has won the victory over sin and death. We know of his resurrection from his appearances to his apostles and disciples.

(1) Jesus appeared to Peter. Peter has a special place in the life of the Church. He was chosen as the Rock upon which Jesus built his Church. He is the leader of the college of apostles. He is the one who often answered the questions of Jesus on behalf of all the apostles.

From the Gospel accounts, we also gather that Peter often spoke impetuously. Later, he learnt from his experiences. One such experience comes to mind, namely, when during the Last Supper Jesus told the apostles about his suffering and death and resurrection.

Jesus said to the apostles, "You will all become deserters; for
it is written, 'I will strike the shepherd, and the sheep will be
scattered.' But after I am raised up, I will go before you to
Galilee." Peter said to him, "Even though all become desert-

ers, I will not." Jesus said to him, "Truly I tell you, this day, this very night, before the cock crows twice, you will deny me three times." But Peter said vehemently, "Even though I must die with you, I will not deny you." And all of them said the same (Mk 14:27-31).

In Mark's account of the Resurrection story, the word of the heavenly messenger who sat in the empty tomb was, "Go, tell his disciples *and Peter* that he is going ahead of you to Galilee; there you will see him, just as he told you" (Mk 16:7, emphasis added). In Luke also the disciples say, "The Lord has risen indeed, and he has appeared to *Simon!*" (Lk 24:34, emphasis added).

It is heartening to see that one of the first appearances of the risen Lord Jesus was to the apostle who had denied him three times (cf. Mk 14:66-72). Jesus' desire was to set Peter free of his guilt-feeling lest it become a big obstacle for the fruitfulness of his apostolic ministry in the future. Jesus knew that Peter had repented with his whole heart and had wept bitterly for his sin of denying Jesus. Peter truly loved Jesus and Jesus loved Peter and did not take back his choice of Peter as the leader of the apostles.

(2) Jesus appeared to Mary Magdalene. She was a disciple of Jesus. Jesus had brought her deliverance from evil oppression. Even though the popular picture given about Mary Magdalene is often that of a loose woman whom Jesus forgave, the biblical account of Mary of Magdala is quite different. The text that introduces her to us is found in Luke, where he says,

The twelve were with him, as well as some women who had been cured of evil spirits and infirmities: Mary, called Magdalene, from whom seven demons had gone out, and Joanna ... and many others, who provided for them out of their resources (Lk 8:1-3).

Mark's Gospel account also tells us that, "he appeared first to Mary Magdalene from whom he had cast out seven demons" (Mk 16:9).

The other places in the Gospel accounts where we find Mary Magdalene are when she stood by the cross (Mt 27:56), watched Jesus' burial (Mt 27:61), came early to the sepulcher (Mt 28:1), and saw the risen Lord (Mt 28:9; Mk 16:9; Jn 20:11-18).

The appearance of the risen Lord Jesus to her is given in detail in John's account. As Mary stood outside the tomb weeping, she did not recognize Jesus when he stood before her and asked her, "Woman, why are you weeping? Whom are you looking for?" But later on when she heard Jesus call her by name, "Mary!" she recognized him and wanted to cling to him and not let him go from her ever again.

But Jesus said to her,

"Do not hold me . . . But go to my brothers and say to them, I am ascending to my Father and your Father, to my God and your God." Mary Magdalene went and announced to the disciples, "I have seen the Lord"; and she told them that he had said these things to her (Jn 20:17-18).

Mary Magdalene is remembered down through history specially because the Risen Lord appeared to her and revealed his resurrection to her. He made her his witness and sent her to the apostles with the message of his resurrection. With Jesus, there is no discrimination between male and female, he reveals himself to all alike.

(3) Jesus appeared to Paul. We hear about it from Paul himself:

Christ . . . appeared to Cephas, then to the twelve . . . Last of all, as to one untimely born, he appeared also to me. For I am the least of the apostles, unfit to be called an apostle, because

I persecuted the church of God" (1 Cor 15:5-9, emphasis added).

The appearance of the risen Lord on the way to Damascus was the most precious moment of Paul's life. It was the moment when Paul's life was turned upside down and inside out, and he was transformed in his inner being from being a persecutor of the church to becoming an apostle of Christ Jesus. From Paul's words we see his utter humility and, at the same time, his consciousness of his own worth in Christ Jesus.

I regard everything as loss because of the surpassing value of knowing Christ Jesus my Lord . . . I want to know Christ and the power of his resurrection and the sharing of his sufferings by becoming like him in his death, if somehow I may attain the resurrection of the dead (Phil 3:8-11).

Let us all together celebrate the victory of the Risen Lord over sin and death, let us cry out the words of this psalm,

Praise the LORD! Praise God in his sanctuary . . . Praise him for his mighty deeds . . . Let everything that breathes praise the LORD! Praise the LORD!

SEEKING JESUS...

In the Prophets

Explanatory Note

The radiant face of Jesus sheds its light upon us from the Old Testament also through the messages, visions, and actions of the Prophets. Here we reflect only on the writings of the Later Prophets; they not only proclaimed God's messages but also had them written down, starting from Amos and Hosea (c. 786 BCE) to the prophets after the exile, namely Haggai and Zechariah (c. 520-519 BCE).

Actually, there were prophets functioning right from the time of the first king of Israel, such as Samuel in the time of King Saul (1020-1000 BCE), Gad and Nathan in the time of King David (1000-962 BCE), and later Elijah and Elisha in the time of kings Ahab, Ahaziah, Jehoram, Jehoash, (c. 875-795 BCE), and many others, including Deborah, a woman prophet and judge in Israel (cf. Judg 4: 4-5:15). However, their prophecies have not been handed down to us in separate written books, but are part of the Historical Books of the Old Testament.

All the prophets belong to Jewish history, those speaking during the reign of kings first in the united kingdom of Israel, and later in the divided kingdoms of Israel and Judah, and even later when, after the Babylonian exile, there no longer existed the northern kingdom Israel or the southern kingdom Judah, but both were one country, Palestine (under foreign rulers).

It is beyond the scope of this work, which is meant primarily for spiritual nourishment and contemplation, to treat exegetical details from the Historical Books. Similarly, the books constituting Wisdom Literature (a collection of books from various historical periods, approximately from the time of the court schools during the reign of Solomon, i.e. 962 BCE, till the 1st century BCE), will also not be treated in this work.

Suffice it to note that the Book of the Wisdom of Solomon describes wisdom as God's creative word (Wis 9:1) and the "breath of the power of God" (Wis 7:25). The sage longs for this breath of God's creative word saying, "Who has learned thy counsel, unless thou hast given wisdom and sent thy holy Spirit from on high?" (Wis 9:17).

The Prophet Isaiah

ISAIAH 6:9-10

Go, and say to this people: "Hear and hear, but do not understand; see and see, but do not perceive." Make the heart of this people fat, and their ears heavy, and shut their eyes; lest they see with their eyes, and hear with their ears, and understand with their hearts, and turn and be healed.

If we read these words without attention to the context in which they were said, or if we read them superficially, we may wrongly conclude that God does not want his people to listen to his words and be healed! However, from our experience of the loving and merciful God, we know that God delights in us, and desires our wholehearted attention. The very purpose of sending his prophet to his people was to make the people hear, heed and obey his message. Hence, these words of God through Isaiah must have a deeper meaning than appears at first sight.

The words, "Make the heart of this people fat, and their ears heavy, and shut their eyes," in themselves give us a clue to what is implied in the message. We may easily attest, from our own experience, that when someone, especially someone in authority, gives a word of correction or direction, then among the listeners, those who are stubborn and fixed in their selfish ways, resist and do not want to listen. Their hearts are not supple and sincere, nor are their ears open to the word of the Lord, hence their ears become heavy so that they actually hear nothing of the correction, nor see any sense because any word of reproof and correction becomes a burden for them, it becomes like water splashed on a duck's back.

We know how on countless occasions God pleaded with his people to heed his words and keep his commands in order to become holy and acceptable to God, and a light for all peoples and nations around them. But again and again we also see how the people took God for granted, and treated his words very lightly, continuing to do whatever pleased them. We come across a good illustration of this in the words uttered by a psalmist in prayer,

> *Hear, O my people, while I admonish you!*
> *O Israel, if you would but listen to me!*
> *. . . But my people did not listen to my voice; Israel would have*
>   *none of me . . .*
> *O that my people would listen to me, that Israel would walk*
>   *in my ways! (Ps 81:8-16).*

The Lord spoke in similar manner through the prophet Jeremiah, saying, "From the day that your fathers came out of the land of Egypt to this day, I have persistently sent all my servants the prophets to them, day after day; yet they did not listen to me, or incline their ear, but stiffened their neck" (Jer 7:25-28).

Therefore, what God wants to communicate through the prophet Isaiah is just the opposite of what the words seem to say. It is not God who desires that the ears and eyes of the people become deaf and blind, nor does God want to stop them from turning to him and receiving healing. On the contrary, God wants them to listen and see and turn from their stubbornness of heart, and repent and be healed.

But the people's hearts are stubborn and they do not want to turn to God for guidance. Only when some calamity descends on them personally or as a community, then they cry out to God for deliverance, at all other times when they seemingly are doing fine, they forget the loving and merciful God who alone gives them all the good things that they have and enjoy. I am sure that often we can also recognize our own behavior in the conduct of the stubborn people of God.

Jesus told the crowds the parable of the seed and the sower. After he had told the parable, his disciples asked him what the parable meant. Before explaining it to them, Jesus said,

> To you it has been given to know the secrets of the kingdom of God; but for others they are in parables, so that seeing they may not see, and hearing they may not understand (Lk 8:10).

Again, a quick and superficial reading of these words of Jesus may give the impression that Jesus wanted only his disciples to understand what he meant. But it is clear that Jesus spoke in parables, the language of story telling, so that all the people could easily understand and respond to the message.

Jesus explains that he teaches about the secrets of the kingdom in parables to those who are not yet his disciples. This is because they were not as advanced, perhaps, as the disciples were, in the knowledge of spiritual realities. The disciples lived with Jesus, listened to him, ate with him, and were in constant contact with him. Thus, they learnt more from Jesus than the crowds did. The words of Jesus had attracted them to join the family of disciples. They had made a choice for Jesus.

But among the crowds that followed Jesus, many people came only to hear him, to be fed by him and to be healed of their diseases. They had not made a definite choice for Jesus. They had not accepted discipleship. They were only following him wherever he went because there were many benefits from it. Later Jesus addressed the crowds and invited them to stop vacillating and to make a definite choice to be with him.

Jesus said to the crowds, "When you see a cloud rising in the west; you immediately say, It is going to rain; and so it happens. And when you see the south wind blowing, you say, There will be scorching heat; and it happens. You hypocrites! You know how to interpret the appearance of earth and sky, but why do you not know how to interpret the present time?" (Lk 12:54-56).

In another place Jesus says of the crowds,

To what then will I compare the people of this generation, and what are they like? They are like children sitting in the marketplace and calling to one another, "we played the flute for you, and you did not dance; we wailed, and you did not weep" (Lk 7:31-32).

The crowds accompany Jesus to see signs and wonders, they are not ready to make any choice either for or against Jesus. These were the same people who had also heard John the Baptist calling them to change their hearts from evil and believe in the Lord, but they did not listen to him. In similar fashion, they did not listen to Jesus who walked among them, teaching, feeding, healing, and laying down his life for them.

Such people's hearts are lukewarm and hardened, their ears are heavy and eyes are shut, so that they do not wish to listen, believe and obey the commands of the loving Savior. They refuse the cost of discipleship. These are the people who, when they meet with trials and adversities in life, are very quick to blame God for their condition.

Let us examine our own hearts and see whether this is sadly true of us also. Especially we, who are baptized Christians and who come to receive the sacraments, let us ask ourselves: are our spiritual lives lukewarm or dry and fruitless? If we are in the habit of responding to God like the morning dew which comes now and disappears soon after, then today let us turn away from our fickle-mindedness, and turn to God our Father immediately, for the word says,

> *Draw near to God and he will draw near to you . . . Humble yourself before the Lord, and he will exalt you (Jas 4:8,10).*

The call from God and the challenge from Jesus to us today is that as the Lord God has come to us in Jesus his Son, so we must come back to him with sincere hearts believing in Jesus. And let our faith be accompanied by our obedience to the commands of the Lord, because Jesus says, "If you love me, you will keep my commandments" (Jn 14:15). Our faith and love must be made manifest in the good works that we do towards neighbor and society:

> *Those who say, "I love God," and hate their brothers or sisters, are liars; for those who do not love a brother or sister whom they have seen, cannot love God whom they have not seen (1 Jn 4:20).*

ISAIAH 7:14

Behold, a young woman shall conceive and bear a son, and shall call his name Immanuel.

The prophet Isaiah spoke these words to King Ahaz of Judah who was putting greater trust in his own wisdom, and not in the Lord God. Isaiah assured Ahaz that the Lord God alone could deliver him and his people from the hands of invading powers (cf. Is 7:2-9). But the king did not want to heed the prophet's words, instead he offered a sly answer, making it sound very proper: "I will not put the LORD to the test" (Is 7:12). The fact was that he had already decided what he would do (namely, make an alliance with the stronger invading power, Assyria, against the two invaders, namely the northern kingdom, Israel and its ally, Syria).

Ahaz did not want God's will to interfere with his own decision. In practical terms, for Ahaz, Assyria had greater power than the Lord God.

Even though his heart was not right with God, yet God could not forget his covenant with his People. God himself wanted to give his people a sign to sustain their hope and strength in the face of impending war. God called them, through the prophet, to depend totally on his power to save. The king did not obey God's word, nor did he think about the people's good, he did what the world and his fear dictated. Nevertheless, God in his mercy promised a future king, in the time of the prophet. This would be King Hezekiah, who, unlike his father, was a God-fearing and reforming king. He would bring fresh breath and hope to the people. The promise of the Lord was that,

> *before the child knows how to refuse the evil and choose the good, the land before whose two kings you are in dread, will be deserted (Is 7:16).*

When Matthew wrote his account of the Gospel mainly for a Jewish Christian audience, he consistently made reference to the words from the Old Testament that spoke about the messiah, and demonstrated how Jesus was this Messiah. He tells us about Joseph's dilemma and God's response to him:

> As he considered this, behold, an angel of the Lord appeared to him in a dream, saying, "Joseph, son of David, do not fear to take Mary your wife, for that which is conceived in her is of the Holy Spirit; she will bear a son, and you shall call his name Jesus, for he will save his people from their sins." All this took place to fulfill what the Lord had spoken by the prophet: "Behold, a virgin shall conceive and bear a son, and his name shall be called Emmanuel" (which means, God with us) (Mt 1:20-23).

In St. Matthew's writings, the two names of the Messiah, Jesus and Emmanuel, are inter-connected. Jesus means "God saves," and Emmanuel means "God with us." Jesus is God with us who saves from sin, evil, and eternal death. Let us look at these names more closely.

(1) "You shall call his name Jesus, for he will save his people from their sins" (Mt 1:21).

Jesus saves. Jesus saves us from evil. Jesus saves us from sin. And along with sins Jesus also frees us from the effects of sin in our lives and gives us grace to overcome temptation and sin. Jesus is our Salvation.

In Capernaum, Jesus was preaching the word, while he sat in a house crowded with people. So many people were there, "that there was no longer room for them, not even about the door." And four men, friends of a paralytic, who believed in Jesus, brought the paralytic to Jesus for healing. But they could not get anywhere close to Jesus. So they climbed the roof and, "removed the roof above him, and when they had made an opening, they let down the pallet on which the paralytic lay. And when Jesus saw their faith, he said to the paralytic, 'My son, your sins are forgiven.'"

The scribes, who were teachers of the Law, were upset at what Jesus had said, they questioned in their hearts saying: "How can this man forgive sins, he is blaspheming." They may have accepted just the physical healing of the paralytic, but they could not accept the spiritual healing that Jesus gave by forgiving sins. They sternly held that only the Almighty God whom they worshipped as Yahweh could forgive sins.

Jesus knew in his spirit that they were questioning within themselves. So he said to them,

> *"Why do you question thus in your hearts? . . . But that you may know that the Son of man has authority on earth to forgive sins,"* — he said to the paralytic — *"I say to you, rise, take up your pallet and go home." And he rose, and immediately took up the pallet and went out before them all. The paralytic got up, not only healed but also strengthened so that he could pick up his pallet and go out before them all; so that they were all amazed and glorified God , saying "We never saw anything like this!" (Mk 2:8-12).*

(2) "His name shall be called Emmanuel, (which means, God with us)" (Mt 1:23).

Jesus is Emmanuel. In the person of Jesus, God is with us. He is our sure hope as the "Amen" to all God's promises. Whenever we hear Jesus saying, "I am with you," he includes the Father and the Holy Spirit as being one with him. Jesus is never separated from the Father and the Spirit. The Spirit makes us aware of the presence of Jesus and the Father. Jesus declares, "The Father and I are one" (Jn 10:30).

Jesus says, "Those who love me will keep my word, and my Father will love them, and we will come to them and make our home with them" (Jn 14:23).

When we look at the several covenants that God made with his People, we see that these involved commitment not from God's side alone but also from the People's side. God said, "Obey my voice, and I will be your God, and you shall be my people . . . But they did not obey or incline their ear, but walked in their own counsels and stubbornness of their hearts, and went backward and not forward" (Jer 7:23-24).

Even though the People promised God saying, "All that the LORD has spoken, we will do" (Ex 19:8), they did not keep their promise. God was always present with them, but they were most of the time far away from him, both in their minds and their behavior.

We Christians proclaim that Jesus is Emmanuel, God with us. Jesus too made an everlasting covenant with us, a covenant in his "blood shed and body broken" for us. Each time when we participate in the celebration of the Holy Eucharist we must remind ourselves of this covenant and of our own commitment to believe in his word, to keep his word not only in our hearts but also in our day-to-day practical lives and relationships. His precious sacramental body and blood is Jesus himself coming to us each day, as we utter the "Amen" before receiving him. This is not our response to Jesus only, but it is also a commitment that we make to Jesus.

Nonetheless, how much of this reality do we consciously believe and accept? Perhaps after having received Jesus on our tongues or hands, we still use our tongues to utter abusive language and our hands for violence toward others and ourselves. We believe Jesus is God with us, but how often do we behave as if we are the sole authority to make all the decisions for our lives and for those of our families and others. How often do we consult Jesus in prayer?

Although the beautiful fact is that Jesus is Emmanuel, God-with-us, the question we must ask ourselves today is: *am I* also with him? He takes delight in our presence with him as much as (even more than) we do in his presence with us. Let us humbly recall how much attention we really give him while praying, either alone or in the Church. How many distractions and daydreams flood our minds when we sit down to pray even the family rosary? These are our weak moments, but we must try harder to take Jesus and his love for us seriously. He waits. He knocks. He will not force his way in. Let us respond now!

St. Teresa of Ávila taught that if one prays for a long time, but without attention, one has not prayed at all. Therefore, today, let us make a renewed effort to respond to Jesus sincerely by giving him our total attention, for as little or as long a time each day that we can. He does not look for perfect disciples, rather, he makes us perfect as we express our longing for him with childlike faith and openness.

ISAIAH 9:6-7a

For to us a child is born, to us a son is given; and the government will be upon his shoulder, and his name will be called "Wonderful Counselor, Mighty God, Everlasting Father, Prince of Peace." Of the increase of his government and of peace, there will be no end.

This passage speaks not so much about the birth of a son as about the coronation of a king. As Psalm 2:7 says, "I will tell of the decree of the LORD: He said to me, 'You are my son, today I have begotten you'" This begetting is at the same time the king's coronation, when authority will be laid on his shoulders and he will begin to reign.

Jesus was crowned as everlasting king especially at his victorious rising from the dead. Jesus' reign is in the hearts of people who believe in him, and he reigns over all the earth and sky, seas and winds. Jesus is Lord of all.

During his public ministry, Jesus fulfilled all the above names recorded by Isaiah. He was compassionate as a father toward his children. He was the wonderful counselor whose words brought healing, deliverance, and freedom from every evil. He brought peace and joy into the lives of all those who cried out to him in their need. He brought peace to the whole universe and to all creation, for example, to the turbulent waters of the sea. He said to the sea, "Peace! Be still! And the wind ceased, and there was a great calm" (Mk 4:39).

Jesus wanted so much to bring peace to the land of Jerusalem, the land where God was especially present in the temple and among his people. But the religious and political leaders in the city did not believe in Jesus' words. In fact, they were so jealous of him that they wanted to kill him. Jesus wept over Jerusalem and said,

Jerusalem, Jerusalem, the city that kills the prophets and stones those who are sent to it! How often have I desired to

gather your children together as a hen gathers her brood under
her wings, and you were not willing! See your house is left to
you. And I tell you, you will not see me until the time comes
when you say, "Blessed is the one who comes in the name of
the Lord" (Lk 13:34-35).

Jesus is the Prince of Peace who says to the disciples, "Peace I
leave with you; my peace I give to you. I do not give to you as the
world gives. Do not let your hearts be troubled, and do not let them
be afraid" (Jn 14:27).

The Angel Gabriel announced God's message to Mary, saying,

Jesus . . . will be great, and will be called the Son of the Most
High, and the Lord God will give to him the throne of his
ancestor David. He will reign over the house of Jacob forever,
and of his kingdom there will be no end (Lk 1:31-33).

Let us draw consolation and joy in the fact that the kingdom
of Jesus is everlasting, it has no end, because, "Jesus Christ is the
same yesterday and today and forever" (Heb 13:7).

Jesus is our Advocate who promised us another Counselor,
whom the Father would send, the Holy Spirit, the Paraclete (Jn
14:25-26). The later words of the prophet Isaiah about the Suffering Servant of God illustrate for us the quality of our wonderful
counselor Jesus, who often told his disciples that he said only
what the Father wanted him to say (cf. Jn 14:10):

The LORD God has given me the tongue of a teacher, that I may
know how to sustain the weary with a word. Morning by
morning he wakens my ear to listen as those who are taught
(Is 50:4).

Jesus reigns in our hearts as a loving father reigns in the heart
of his children. Jesus watches over us, nourishes us with his word

and sustains us with his teachings. Jesus shows us the way to the heavenly Father and also reveals him to us. His power is that of the Mighty God who is not like other man-made gods. This is why Moses could encourage the people saying, "what other great nation has a god so near to it as the LORD our God is whenever we call to him?" (Deut 4:7).

Jesus is the Mighty God who is always near us and with us. When we find ourselves in stormy situations of life, we can hear him tell us to not be afraid, that he is with us; "I will not leave you desolate; I will come to you" (Jn 14:18).

The prophet Isaiah also speaks beautiful words of love from God. These words can be heard in many ways in the compassionate ministry of Jesus:

> Can a woman forget her nursing child, or show no compassion for the child of her womb? Even these may forget, yet I will not forget you. See, I have inscribed you on the palms of my hands (Is 49:15-16).

Let us, therefore, take a moment and turn to Jesus with gratitude and love in our hearts, knowing that he is so close to us that we have no need to doubt his presence with us.

ISAIAH 50:5-7

The Lord God has opened my ear, and I was not rebellious, I did not turn backward. I gave my back to those who struck me, and my cheeks to those who pulled out the beard; I did not hide my face from insult and spitting. The Lord God helps me; therefore I have not been disgraced; therefore I have set my face like flint, and I know that I shall not be put to shame; he who vindicates me is near.

(1) "The Lord God has opened my ear, and I was not rebellious." These words apply perfectly to Jesus, whose heart and ears were always open to his Father's voice. He listened to the Father's word and was always obedient to the will of the Father, even when the Father's will was difficult to accept and even when it meant severe suffering and trials for him.

Jesus was quite unlike most of us, who are a lot of the time perhaps rebellious to commands or advice given to us, especially by those in authority over us. Do we not dislike interference with our plans? Do we not seek a comfortable life without any disturbances? This may be the prime reason that we are far from where God our Father wants us to be.

Life offers difficulties and challenges, choices and decisions. In all such situations, our obedience to God's will is the sure way that can bring us joy and fulfillment such as our selfish ideas and plans can never bring. Our ideas and plans, if different from those of God, will leave us unhappy and dissatisfied most of the time. The prophet speaks to God and to the people, saying,

> *Thou dost keep in perfect peace, whose mind is stayed on thee, because he trusts in thee.*
> *Trust in the Lord for ever, for the Lord God is everlasting rock (Is 26:3-4).*

As the Father did not keep any thing hidden from Jesus, so Jesus also revealed everything to his family of disciples. He said to them, "I have called you friends, because I have made known to you everything that I have heard from my Father" (Jn 15:15).

All that Jesus asks of his disciples is that we love him, and loving him means obedience to his commands (cf. Jn 14:15). Jesus loved the Father and obeyed his commands. As the days of his suffering and death drew near, Jesus revealed the Father's plan of salvation to his disciples. Three times he told them about what was awaiting him in Jerusalem, but every time "they did not understand," because they were not ready to understand (cf. Mk 8:32-33). Jesus said to them plainly:

The Son of Man must undergo great suffering, and be rejected by the elders, chief priests, and scribes, and be killed, and on the third day be raised (Lk 9:22).

Let these words sink into your ears: The Son of Man is going to be betrayed into human hands (Lk 9:44).

See, we are going up to Jerusalem, and everything that is written about the Son of Man by the prophets will be accomplished. For he will be handed over to the Gentiles, and he will be mocked and insulted and spat upon. After they have flogged him, they will kill him, and on the third day he will rise again (Lk 18:31-33).

Thus Jesus heard the Father's command and was not rebellious to his plan of salvation which involved going through extreme physical and emotional suffering and a shameful death on the cross. After this, he would be raised from the dead by the Father (cf. Acts 2:32, 3:10). To accomplish the Father's plan, Jesus remained steadfast and was not rebellious when he was tortured, mocked, insulted, treated like a criminal and crucified.

(2) "I have set my face like flint." St. Luke tells us, "When the days drew near for him to be taken up, Jesus set his face to go to Jerusalem" (Lk 9:51).

Jerusalem was the place that had rejected and killed the prophets sent by God (cf. Lk 13:34). Jesus knew that he too would be rejected by its chief priests, elders and scribes, yet, he was determined to go up to Jerusalem, because it was the place where he would glorify the Father through his saving death and resurrection. After Jesus prayed earnestly to the Father on the Mount of Olives, and surrendered his will to the Father's will, nothing could keep him from taking up the cross, carrying it up to Calvary, being nailed to the cross and dying on it like a criminal.

(3) "I gave my back to those who struck me . . . I did not hide my face from insult and spitting."

Many centuries before Jesus, the prophet Isaiah's first reference here was to the people of God, who had suffered greatly during the exile. But in Jesus' sufferings, we can see the prophet's words taking on full meaning and significance.

After Pilate washed his hands, to satisfy the crowds, he had Jesus flogged, and then he handed him over to be crucified.

> Then the soldiers led him into the courtyard of the palace; and they called together the whole cohort. And they clothed him in a purple cloak; and after twisting some thorns into a crown they put it on him. And they began saluting him, "Hail, King of the Jews!" They struck his head with a reed, spat upon him, and knelt down in homage to him. After mocking him, they stripped him (Mk 15:15-20).

(4) "The Lord GOD helps me; therefore I have not been disgraced . . . he who vindicates me is near."

As Jesus hung on the cross, the rulers and soldiers continued to mock and taunt him, saying, "He saved others; let him save himself... If you are the King of the Jews, save yourself!" (Lk 23:35-37). But Jesus, trusting in his Father alone, said, "Father, forgive them; for they know not what they do."

Jesus knew that even though in the eyes of his persecutors he was a blasphemer and a criminal, and many of his own disciples were confused about him, yet, his heavenly Father was on his side. He would not allow Jesus his Son to be disgraced. With confidence in the Father's closeness, Jesus cried out with a loud voice, "Father, into your hands I commit my spirit!" (Lk 23:34, 46). Jesus entrusted his spirit to the Father and breathed his last.

The apostle Paul received from the Spirit of Jesus a similar confidence:

> But I am not ashamed, for I know the one in whom I have put my trust, and I am sure that he is able to guard until that day what I have entrusted to him (2 Tim 1:12).

The "day" is the time when Jesus will come again, with all dominion and power. Stephen gave testimony to this when he was on trial before the very same Sanhedrin that had tried Jesus also:

> Filled with the Holy Spirit, Stephen gazed into heaven and saw the glory of God and Jesus standing at the right hand of God. "Look," he said, "I see the heavens opened and the Son of Man standing at the right hand of God!" (Acts 7:55-56).

ISAIAH 52:13 – 53:12

This text is called the fourth Song of the Suffering Servant of God. (The other three Songs of the Servant of God are: Isaiah 42:1-4; 49:1-6; and 50:4-9.) While reading the passage, we are led to meditate deeply on the passion, death and exaltation of Jesus Christ,

> *Who, though he was in the form of God, did not regard equality with God as something to be grasped, but emptied himself, taking the form of a servant, being born in the likeness of men. And being found in human form, he humbled himself and became obedient unto death, even death on a cross. Therefore God has highly exalted him and bestowed on him the name which is above every name, that at the name of Jesus every knee should bow, in heaven and on earth and under the earth, and every tongue confess that Jesus Christ is Lord, to the glory of God the Father (Phil 2:6-11).*

When we read this hymn of the self-emptying of Jesus Christ, written by St. Paul, and then read the above text of the prophet Isaiah, we notice that Isaiah begins by talking about the exaltation and the glory of the Servant of God. This glory is bestowed on him by God because of the depth of his humility and self-emptying in obedience to God's will for, "through him the will of the LORD shall prosper" (Is 53:10b). The speaker in this text is God who is proudly presenting his faithful Servant to all nations, but especially to those who believe in him.

> (1) *Behold, my servant shall prosper, he shall be exalted and lifted up and shall be very high. As many were astonished at him, his appearance was so marred, beyond human semblance, and his form beyond that of the sons of men, so shall he startle many nations; kings shall shut their mouths because of him; for that which has not been told them they shall see,*

and that which they have not heard they shall understand (Is 52:13-15).

It is only after the Lord's resurrection, ascension, and sending of the Spirit at Pentecost that those who had heard and believed the words of Jesus received clear understanding about all that Jesus had said and done in his public ministry, his passion, death and resurrection, and ascension. And they became his witnesses to all the nations, even to the ends of the earth, just as Jesus had promised, saying:

You will receive power when the Holy Spirit has come upon you; and you will be my witnesses in Jerusalem, in all Judea and Samaria, and to the end of the earth (Acts 1:8).

Jesus went about among the people, spoke with them, taught the crowds about the kingdom of God and performed works of power, yet, St. John tells us that:

Although he had performed so many signs in their presence, they did not believe in him. This was to fulfill the word spoken by the prophet Isaiah: "Lord, who has believed our message, and to whom has the arm of the Lord been revealed?" And so they could not believe (Jn 12:37-39, Is 53:1).

(2) The Servant Song goes on:

He was despised and rejected by men; a man of sorrows, and acquainted with grief; and as one from whom people hide their faces he was despised, and we esteemed him not. Surely he has borne our griefs and carried our sorrows; yet we esteemed him stricken, smitten by God, and afflicted. But he was wounded for our transgressions, he was bruised for our iniquities; upon him was the chastisement that made us whole, and with his stripes we are healed" (Is 53:3-5).

He was despised and rejected. From the very beginning of his public ministry, Jesus was despised and rejected even by the people of his own village. Let us recall the day when after his baptism in the Jordan and temptations in the wilderness, Jesus came to his hometown Nazareth. He went to the synagogue and did the reading from the scroll of the prophet Isaiah. After reading he began to say, "Today this scripture has been fulfilled in your hearing" (Lk 4:16-21). Those gathered in the synagogue did not want to listen to him, they were filled with rage at what he said.

They got up, drove him out of the town, and led him to the brow of the hill on which their town was built, so that they might hurl him off the cliff (Lk 4:29).

All through the weeks, months, and years that Jesus taught in their synagogues, in market-places and squares, on the hills and seashores, on the mountains and the plains, in desert regions and in the temple courts, many people believed in him and became his disciples, but there were many who followed him only because Jesus met their physical needs, and there were also many, especially the scribes and Pharisees, who took every chance to attack everything he said and did. They could not become his real disciples. The scribes were even more dangerous because of their alliance with the chief priests and elders, they despised and rejected Jesus from the very beginning of Jesus' ministry until his death, and even after his death they wanted to quash the good news of the resurrection.

"A man of sorrows, and acquainted with grief." Once, when Jesus was in Jerusalem at the Passover feast, many people believed in his name because they saw the wonderful works that he did. They even wanted to "take him by force to make him king," after he had fed the crowds (cf. Jn 6:15). But Jesus, who was "acquainted with grief," withdrew to the mountain by himself. He was not taken in by their false exaltation of him. St. John tells us:

> *Jesus did not trust himself to them, because he knew all men and needed no one to bear witness of man; for he himself knew what was in man (Jn 2:23-25).*

Jesus knows what is in us, he knows our thoughts and intentions from afar. Still he cares for us. Such is his love and forbearance toward us. He never complains to his Father about us, nor does he stop walking with us. His wisdom and love can never be measured and his patience has no limits.

"Surely he has borne our griefs, yet we esteemed him stricken, smitten by God." After Jesus was betrayed by his apostle Judas Iscariot, and arrested by the chief priests, the officers of the temple police, and the elders, they led him into the high priest's house, and then brought him before the council. There they all condemned Jesus for blasphemy (cf. Lk 22:47-72). The prescribed punishment for blasphemy was death. All the days and weeks that they had observed Jesus, heard his teachings and seen his works, these religious leaders kept their hearts closed to the message of God. For them Jesus was one cursed by God who deserved death by a shameful crucifixion: "Cursed is everyone who hangs on a tree" (cf. Gal 3:13).

> *But he was wounded for our transgressions, he was bruised for our iniquities; upon him was the chastisement that made us whole, and with his stripes we are healed (Is 53:5).*

It was God's saving plan of love, right from the time of the fall of Adam and Eve, that he would redeem his sinful children through the Saviour who would crush the head of the serpent. The devil is also called the deceiver (Rev 12:9) and the accuser (Rev 12:10), who leads us to sin and death (cf. Gen 3:15).

Jesus, the only begotten Son of God, the Holy and Righteous One (Acts 3:14), is the Redeemer through whom God saved the world out of the hands of the evil one. Whatever rejection, pain, shame, and evil Jesus suffered at the hands of lawless men, even unto death on the cross, he suffered it all for our sake. "With his stripes we are healed." Thus, St. Paul cries out,

> O the depth of the riches and wisdom and knowledge of God!
> How unsearchable are his judgments and how inscrutable his
> ways! ... To him be glory for ever. Amen (Rom 11:33).

St. John explains about the redemptive plan of God our Father who sent his only Son to suffer and to die so that we might have life in all its fullness:

> For God so loved the world that he gave his only Son, that
> whoever believes in him should not perish but have eternal
> life. For God sent the Son into the world, not to condemn the
> world, but that the world might be saved through him (Jn
> 3:16-17).

Whatever Jesus taught or commanded his disciples to do, he first lived out in his own life. He did not teach like the scribes and Pharisees who taught but did not practice their own teachings. Jesus taught the quality of true and sublime love, and he showed it in action too.

> Greater love has no man than this, that a man lay down his
> life for his friends (Jn 15:13).

God laid "upon him the iniquity of us all and upon him was the chastisement that made us whole" (Is 53:5-6). So with all the angels and saints let us sing a new song, saying,

Worthy are you O Lamb, for you were slain and by your blood you have ransomed us for God from every tribe and tongue and people and nation (Rev 5:9).

(3) When Judas Iscariot betrayed Jesus with a treacherous kiss, those who came to arrest Jesus seized him. Immediately, one of Jesus' disciples drew out a sword and struck the slave of the high priest and cut off his ear. Then Jesus said to him,

Put your sword back into its place; for all who take the sword will perish by the sword. Do you think that I cannot appeal to my Father, and he will at once send me more than twelve legions of angels? But how then should the scriptures be fulfilled, that it must be so? (Mt 26:47-54).

Being interested in fulfilling the Father's plan of salvation for us, Jesus did not appeal to the Father to protect him from the violence that his enemies would do to him. This was foretold by the prophet Isaiah,

He was oppressed, and he was afflicted, yet he opened not his mouth; like a lamb that is led to the slaughter, and like a sheep that before its shearers is dumb, so he opened not his mouth (Is 53:7).

During his Sermon on the Mount (Mt 5-7), Jesus taught his disciples about the qualities of a believer who is truly blessed. Jesus taught the Beatitudes, in which he made his will known to us. The beatitudes are like spiritual principles that we must follow in our lives if we wish to become like Jesus.

In the silence of Jesus, while he was being led to the "slaughter," we can recognize a combination of all the beatitudes (cf. Mt 5:3-10), and a determination to accomplish all that the Father asked of him for our salvation.

The Song of the Suffering Servant continues,

Yet it was the will of the LORD to bruise him . . . when he makes himself an offering for sin, he shall prolong his days; the will of the LORD shall prosper in his hand; he shall see the fruit of the travail of his soul and be satisfied; by his knowledge shall the righteous one, my servant, make many to be accounted righteous (Is 53:10-11).

Jesus said to the disciples, "My food is to do the will of him who sent me, and to accomplish his work" (Jn 4:34; cf. Jn 5:30; 6:38). And Isaiah says that it was the will of the Lord God to bruise him. And his wounds heal us. This was the marvelous plan of redemption for which Jesus gave up his life for us. As he hung on the cross he knew that he had done all that the Father had sent him into the world to do, so he said, "it is accomplished" (Jn 19:30).

Jesus plumbed the depths of the abyss. In his agony and pain, under the burden of the evil built up by the sins of every generation of humanity, he even experienced mysteriously a kind of rupture of relationship with God, of the kind that sin brings. Jesus felt abandonment by the Father on the cross and he cried out, "My God, my God, why have you forsaken me" (Mk 15:34). This was the ultimate moment of the self-emptying of Jesus, caused by his identifying vicariously with all of sinful humanity.

But because of this *kenosis*, because Jesus experienced forsakenness even by his Father, who was otherwise ever close to him, and death on a cross, St. Paul writes about the very happy ending:

Therefore, God has highly exalted him and bestowed on him the name which is above every name, that at the name of Jesus every knee should bow, in heaven and on earth and under the earth, and every tongue confess that Jesus Christ is Lord, to the glory of God the Father (Phil 2:12).

The Prophet Jeremiah

JEREMIAH 11:15-16, 19, 20

What right has my beloved in my house, when she has done vile deeds? . . . The LORD once called you, "A green olive tree, fair with goodly fruit"; but with the roar of a great tempest he will set fire to it, and its branches will be consumed.

(1) The People in whom the Lord God delighted and to whom God had given all his blessings had become ugly with sin and self-ishness. They had rejected their God and Creator; they had separated themselves from God and joined themselves to other gods of their own making. They broke the covenant relationship with God their Father (cf. Jer 3:19), and became wicked, lawless perverts, and merciless, unjust, and bloodthirsty oppressors. They listened with itching ears to the false prophets and did what was evil in the eyes of the loving God (cf. Jer 7:5-7).

With the weight of the cross heavy upon his shoulders, Jesus was being led up to Calvary by the cruel soldiers, mocking elders of the people, and the crowds. The cross he carried was the terrible burden of the sins and evils of all of humanity. Jesus bore these in the form of the shameful cross, as Isaiah had written,

Surely he has borne our infirmities . . . he was wounded for our transgressions . . . he was numbered with transgressors, yet he . . . made intercession for the transgressors (Is 53:4-5, 12).

Jeremiah says that the Lord had called his people "A green olive tree, fair with goodly fruit," but they had become like dry wood. Let us see the significance of the green wood and the dry wood in the words of Jesus. On the Way of the Cross:

> *A great number of the people followed him, and among them were women who were beating their breasts and wailing for him. But Jesus turned to them and said, "Daughters of Jerusalem, do not weep for me, but weep for yourselves and for your children. For the days are coming when they will say . . . to the mountains, 'Fall on us'; and to the hills, 'Cover us.' For if they do this when the wood is green, what will happen when it is dry?" (Lk 23:28-31).*

The tree that dries up and stops bearing any good fruit deserves only to be cut down and burnt. This is why the prophet says that, "with the roar of a great tempest he will set fire to it, and its branches will be consumed." However, the punishment that the people deserved was not given to *them*, rather, Jesus took upon himself the sins of all and suffered our punishment.

Jesus is the green wood, he is the fruitful tree with healing in its leaves, he is the innocent and beautiful life-giving tree. The dry wood that bears only thorns is the sinful human race, you and I included, that deserves to be punished and burnt up. But, "God is love," and

> *God's love was revealed among us in this way: God sent his only Son into the world so that we might live through him (1 Jn 4:8-9).*

In accordance with the Father's loving plan of salvation, Jesus took upon himself all the dryness, stubbornness, fruitlessness, and ugliness of the dry black wood and offered himself up as a sin offering for the atonement of all.

> For our sake God made him to be sin who knew no sin, so that in him we might become the righteousness of God (2 Cor 5:21).

(2) Jeremiah continues,

> I was like a gentle lamb led to the slaughter . . . they devised schemes, saying, "Let us destroy the tree with its fruit, let us cut him off from the land of the living, so that his name will no longer be remembered!" (Jer 11:19).

And they did so. They put Jesus to death on the cross, they thought that was the end of him and that at last they had gotten rid of him. On the contrary, let us hear the loud words of Peter, the Apostle, proclaiming the truth to all,

> You rejected the Holy and Righteous One and . . . you killed the Author of life, but God raised him from the dead. To this we are witnesses (Acts 3:14-15).

(3) Foreshadowing Jesus, the prophet Jeremiah suffered greatly for speaking out the true message of God to the people. He suffered from kings, from priests, from false prophets, from the people and also from his own family. Hence, he too was like a lamb led to the slaughter. Many times he had to flee from place to place, he was beaten, thrown into a well, kept chained in prison cells, and his prophecies that God commanded him to write down were burnt by the king (cf. Jer 36:23ff). And he had to write them down again.

Jeremiah often interceded with God on behalf of the people, but sometimes he would get very discouraged and cry out to the Lord to punish them (for example, Jer 18:18-23), saying,

But you, O LORD of hosts, who judge righteously, who try the heart and the mind, let me see your retribution upon them, for to you I have committed my cause (Jer 11:20).

Turning our gaze to the compassionate face of Jesus, we will see that Jesus is quite unlike Jeremiah in this regard. For even in the depths of his pain and forsakenness he continued to intercede for his enemies. Hanging from the cross, Jesus said,

Father, forgive them; for they do not know what they are doing (Lk 23:34).

When we are assailed with sorrows and difficulties brought to us by others, let us choose to be like Jesus who forgave us without any conditions. And let us pray for those who afflict us. Then we will bring a smile to the face of Jesus and joy to our own hearts too.

JEREMIAH 31:31-34

The days are surely coming, says the LORD, when I will make a new covenant with the house of Israel ... It will not be like the covenant that I made with their ancestors ... a covenant which they broke. But this is the covenant that I will make with them: I will put my law within them, and I will write it on their hearts; and I will be their God, and they shall be my people. No longer shall they teach one another, or say to each other, "Know the LORD," for they shall all know me, from the least of them to the greatest, says the LORD; for I will forgive their iniquity, and remember their sin no more.

(1) In Christ Jesus, God has made this new covenant with us. Jesus sealed this covenant with his own blood poured out for us and for our redemption. The letter to the Hebrews explains this:

Christ entered once for all into the Holy Place, not with the blood of goats and calves, but with his own blood, thus obtaining eternal redemption ... For this reason he is the mediator of a new covenant, so that those who are called may receive the promised eternal inheritance, because a death has occurred that redeems them from the transgressions under the first covenant (Heb 9:11-15; cf. also 12:24).

Jesus explains this clearly by his word and action during the Last Supper with his disciples. We read:

Jesus did the same with the cup after supper, saying, "This cup that is poured out for you is the new covenant in my blood" (Lk 22:20).

St. Matthew's account gives the same words of Jesus but adds that the blood of Jesus was poured out for the forgiveness of sins:

Jesus took a cup, and after giving thanks he gave it to them, saying, "Drink from it, all of you; for this is my blood of the covenant, which is poured out for many for the forgiveness of sins" (Mt 26:27-28).

God said to us through the prophet Jeremiah that by the new covenant he would put his law within us, and would write it on our hearts. Then he said, "I will be their God, and they shall be my people."

In other words, the new covenant reconciles the hearts of people with the heart of God. Jesus becomes the atonement, that is, the forgiveness of sins for our reconciliation with the Father, once and for all, by his whole life culminating in the shedding of his blood on the cross, the blood that sealed the new covenant between God the Father and all his children through Jesus Christ.

When the Father looks at us, he sees in us the loving face of Jesus his only Son, who makes us adopted children of the Father. We inherit eternal life through Jesus our Redeemer. St. Paul boasts about this saving reconciliation with the Father, saying,

If while we were enemies, we were reconciled to God through the death of his Son, much more surely, having been reconciled, will we be saved by his life. But more than that, we even boast in God through our Lord Jesus Christ, through whom we have now received reconciliation (Rom 5:10-11).

(2) The new covenant is written on our hearts. God our Father is interested in writing his new law on our hearts, and no longer on tablets of stone. God is not interested in externals, nor is God attracted by outer looks. The prophet Isaiah tells us that God is drawn to "the one who has a humble and contrite heart, who trembles at [God's] word" (Is 66:2b).

The heart is the center of one's being, a place where we are molded and formed. When we love, we love with the heart, that is, with all our being. When we learn also it is with the heart. Remember how as children and students when we needed to learn something which we did not wish to forget easily, we learnt it "by heart." It is the intentions of the heart that lead us to say and do things, which show up our character and personality.

In the heart a person can be clean or unclean, God-fearing or rebellious. There is an incident in the life of the prophet Ezekiel when some of the leaders of Israel, who were not faithful to God's word, came to the prophet for consultation. The prophet then said,

> *The word of the* LORD *came to me: son of man, these men* have taken their idols into their hearts, *and placed their iniquity as a stumbling block before them . . . Therefore say to the house of Israel, Thus says the* LORD *God: Repent and turn away your faces from all your abominations* (Ezek 14:1-8).

Notice, the idols, abominations and unfaithfulness had entered into their hearts, and they needed to repent and empty their hearts of all these stumbling blocks, so that they could be freed and made new again by the mercy of God.

Jesus said that we cannot become clean or unclean by outer things or by eating with unwashed hands, or even by the things that we eat, because these pass out of us easily, but the things that we hold in our hearts do not pass out easily, in fact they influence our whole attitude to life and relationships, and make us clean or unclean.

> *What comes out of the mouth proceeds from the heart, and this is what defiles. For out of the heart come evil intentions, murder, adultery . . . These are what defile a person, but to eat with unwashed hands does not defile us* (Mt 15:17-20).

This is why Jesus taught in the beatitudes, "Blessed are the pure in heart, for they will see God" (Mt 5:8). Hence, we cannot see

God's hand at work in our lives or in the lives of others if we keep our hearts cluttered with weak faith and negative, evil intentions. This is why the repentant psalmist prays, "Create in me a clean heart, O God, and put a new and right spirit within me" (Ps 51:10).

Through his words and deeds, Jesus was writing the new law of God on the hearts of all people. The words of the prophet Jeremiah: "No longer shall they teach one another, or say to each other, 'Know the LORD,' for they shall all know me, from the least of them to the greatest," find their fulfillment in the ministry of Jesus. Knowledge of God is intimately linked with the forgiveness of sins and purification of the heart.

When Jesus preached the Good News of God's love and his Kingdom, the words of Jesus pierced the hearts of those listeners whose hearts were open to the message of Jesus, and these became his disciples and followed him, although there were also others, who listened and went their ways; their hearts were not open to God's grace, for they were filled with worldly attractions and ambitions.

We see from people's testimonies how they came to know the true God when they listened to Jesus. Among countless examples, one striking example is that of the tax collector Zacchaeus. When he heard Jesus and welcomed him into his home, Zacchaeus' life was totally changed as he received in his heart the knowledge of God's love and his mercy.

Zacchaeus announced to Jesus, "Look, half of my possessions, Lord, I will give to the poor; and if I have defrauded anyone of anything, I will pay back four times as much" (Lk 19:8). Zacchaeus had responded to the law that had been written on his heart by the presence and words of Jesus.

Another striking example is found in the Samaritan woman. She discussed with Jesus about true worship of God, etc, from her mind. At the same time, her heart was not closed to what Jesus was revealing to her. Jesus knew her heart and revealed the knowledge of God's love and mercy to her. Slowly she recognized something more of Jesus, she learned something new from Jesus, and she experienced something she had never experienced before, a freedom of spirit, acceptance, and purity of heart.

She gave her heart to God as she listened to Jesus and accepted him as her Lord. Immediately she went away and openly gave testimony to the knowledge of Jesus who knew her heart and its ways so well.

Many Samaritans believed in Jesus because of her testimony. They also came to Jesus themselves, and "many more believed because of his word. They said to the woman, 'It is no longer because of what you said that we believe, for we have heard for ourselves, and we know that this is truly the Savior of the world'" (Jn 4:39-42).

This knowledge of God is intimately linked with the experience of forgiveness of sins and the knowledge that God remembers our sin no more, and we are truly redeemed. When God sees us he sees in us his own beloved Son Jesus who dealt with sin for ever by allowing himself to be sacrificed for the sins of all humanity, so that,

> If anyone is in Christ, he/she is a new creation: everything old has passed away; see, everything has become new! (2 Cor 5:17).

The Prophet Ezekiel

EZEKIEL 1:1, 26-28

As I was among the exiles by the river Chebar, the heavens were opened, and I saw visions of God . . . And above the firmament over their heads was the likeness of a throne, in appearance like sapphire; and seated above the likeness of a throne was a likeness as it were of a human form. And upward from what had the appearance of his loins I saw as it were gleaming bronze, like the appearance of fire enclosed round about; and downward from what had the appearance of his loins I saw as it were the appearance of fire, and there was brightness round about him. Like the the appearance of the bow that is in the cloud on the day of rain, so was the appearance of the brightness round about. Such was the appearance of the likeness of the glory of the LORD. And when I saw it, I fell upon my face, and I heard the voice of one speaking.

In this passage, the prophet Ezekiel describes his vision of the glory of God. If, with imaginative faith, we try to visualize this vision of the glory of God, we too will be filled with great awe, wonder, and gratitude, and perhaps will want to remain in that awesome heavenly splendor forever, just like the three apostles when they were present at the transfiguration of Jesus Christ.

Whenever the prophets and evangelists describe the glory of the Lord, its appearance is always like fire shining bright. It is a brightness that one cannot look into, except dimly, as if in a cloud. At such an awesome moment, the only response one can give is to bow down and worship, and listen to God's voice speaking from the glorious splendor.

Let us look into the brilliance and the dazzling light of Jesus as he was transfigured on the mountain:

> *Jesus took with him Peter and James and John, and led them up a high mountain apart, by themselves. And he was trans-figured before them, and his clothes became dazzling white, such as no one on earth could bleach them ... Then a cloud overshadowed them, and from the cloud there came a voice, "This is my Son, the Beloved; listen to him!" (Mk 9:2-7).*

The glory of the Lord in these visions is not something just imagined, it is real. The reality comes across when those who have the vision hear a voice directing them about the present and preparing them for the future. Something similar happened when St. Paul met the risen Lord Jesus on the road to Damascus.

> *Now as he was going along and approaching Damascus, sud-denly a light from heaven flashed around him. He fell to the ground and heard a voice ... For three days he was without sight (Acts 9:3-9).*

St. Paul spoke about this experience as an encounter with the risen Lord Jesus, an encounter that changed his heart and mind and his whole life. He speaks about this encounter in his letters (cf. 1 Cor 15:8; 2 Cor 12:1ff). The experience is also described three times in the Acts of the Apostles (e.g. 9:1-22). With that flash of heavenly light, all the old light of his knowledge of God and the law became as darkness to Paul, as he encountered the new brightness of Jesus Christ and heard his voice for the first time in his life.

In giving testimony to this experience of the risen Lord Jesus, Paul says that he experienced the great light from heaven around noon, at midday (Acts 22:6; 26:13). He was struck down and blinded by the tremendous force of brightness of the Sun of righteousness, Jesus Christ, who shone even brighter than the sun in the sky. And Paul could only respond by falling to the ground and listening to the voice speaking from the brightness.

The experiences of both the prophet Ezekiel and St. Paul bring to mind the experience of the great Moses before the glory of the Lord in the burning bush. Again the image is that of fire, but it is fire that does not destroy. Rather, the fire emanating from the Lord's presence is a healing fire that burns up all that is impure and dark, and makes hearts worthy to be in his presence and hear his voice.

All this magnificent glory belonged to Jesus even as he walked among us, but Jesus did not exploit it for worldly gain. Rather, he emptied himself of any thing that would create a distance between him and us. Jesus took the form of a servant and became obedient unto death, death on a cross (cf. Phil 2:6-8). He did allow his glory to be seen briefly on Mount Tabor, where he was transfigured before three of his apostles. There he was in the company of two Old Testament giants, Moses the beloved lawgiver and Elijah the great prophet, signifying that Jesus is the fulfillment and perfection of the law and the prophets.

Until Jesus died and rose from the dead, he did not allow his divine glory to be seen openly, so that the work of salvation for which he was sent would not be misunderstood as something sensational or as some divine power to be exploited in the world.

With the whole work of Jesus accomplished and God having received the perfect sacrifice of his Son for our reconciliation, we are given another vision, a vision of the prophet John, about the completion of God's perfect will:

The throne of God and of the Lamb will be in the (heavenly) city, and his servants will worship him, they will see his face, and his name will be on their foreheads. And there will be no more night; they need no light of lamp or sun, for the Lord God will be their light (Rev 22:3-5).

Yes, we will dwell in the light of the Lord forever! Amen. Let us too fall down with Ezekiel and the holy men and women of the Old Testament, and with all the servants of Jesus in the New Testament, and worship him who alone is worthy to be adored.

EZEKIEL 11:17-20; 36:25-28

Thus says the Lord God: . . . I will give them one heart, and put a new spirit within them; I will remove the heart of stone from their flesh and give them a heart of flesh, so that they may . . . keep my ordinances and obey them. Then they shall be my people, and I will be their God. I will sprinkle clean water upon you, and you shall be clean from all your uncleannesses . . . A new heart I will give you, and a new spirit I will put within you; and I will remove from your body the heart of stone and give you a heart of flesh. And I will put my spirit within you, and make you follow my statutes, and be careful to observe my ordinances . . . and you shall be my people, and I will be your God.

One heart, a new spirit, a heart of flesh to obey the commandments of the LORD. If there's one thing that makes us ugly it is the divisions we create amongst ourselves. When we have negative feelings of hatred and envy in our hearts towards others we become ugly, because we go against God's will that we be of one heart, united in purpose and mind (cf. 1 Cor 1:10b).

To have gentle and forgiving hearts we need a "renewal of our minds" (cf. Rom 12:2), hence, God wishes to give us a new spirit. Our human spirit can discern what is the will of God, what is good and holy, only by the power of the Holy Spirit whom the Father and the Son give to those who ask (cf. Lk 11:13).

The Holy Spirit is God's love given to us to teach us how to obey the ordinances of the Lord. Jesus said, "If you love me, you will keep my commandments" (Jn 14:15). And Jesus knew that left to ourselves we can will no good, therefore Jesus longed to give us the Holy Spirit who would teach us the truth and enable us to obey his commandments of love:

And I will ask the Father, and he will give you another Advocate, to be with you forever. This Spirit of truth . . . will teach you everything, and remind you of all that I have said to you (Jn 14:16-17, 26).

God says, "I will remove from your body the heart of stone and give you a heart of flesh." It is God who takes the initiative to change our wayward and stubborn hearts and make them sensitive and compassionate. God does this through his Spirit who is, "the love of God poured into our hearts" (cf. Rom 5:5). The Spirit brings us to an intimate relationship with God, so that we can confidently cry out, "Abba! Father!"

God says, "I will put my spirit within you, and make you follow my statutes, and you shall be my people, and I will be your God." This is the depth and breadth of God's loving initiative, if only we show ourselves ready to allow him to work in our lives. God in Jesus makes us his own adopted children who will inherit all the blessings of heaven, provided we do not follow in the footsteps of disobedient Adam and Eve, but in the footsteps of Jesus the beloved Son of God. He was obedient to God's will even to death on a cross in order to restore our original dignity and beauty as God's children.

EZEKIEL 18:2-32

What do you mean by repeating this proverb... "The fathers have eaten sour grapes, and the children's teeth are set on edge"? As I live, says the Lord GOD, this proverb shall no more be used by you... Behold, all souls are mine; the soul of the father as well as the soul of the son is mine: the soul that sins shall die.... Yet you say, "Why should not the son suffer for the iniquity of the father?" When the son has done what is lawful and right, and has been careful to observe all my statutes, he shall surely live. The soul that sins shall die. The son shall not suffer for the iniquity of the father, nor the father suffer for the iniquity of the son... Therefore, I will judge you... every one according to his ways... Repent... Cast away from you all the transgressions which you have committed against me, and get yourselves a new heart and a new spirit! Why will you die...? For I have no pleasure in the death of any one, says the Lord GOD; so turn, and live.

This prophet especially speaks about *personal* retribution for sins. Already in the books of the Pentateuch, there is a gradual development of the teaching about retribution for sins, for example in Deut 24:16 where Moses taught:

The fathers shall not be put to death for the children, nor shall the children be put to death for the fathers; every man shall be put to death for his own sin.

The prophet Jeremiah also had given the same message in Jer 31:29-30, saying,

In those days they shall no longer say: "The fathers have eaten sour grapes, and the children's teeth are set on edge." But every one shall die for his own sin; each man who eats sour grapes, his teeth shall be set on edge.

Even after such clear teaching about personal responsibility for sin and the important need for repentance, the people had not taken God's words seriously and held on to their own old belief that if a child was born blind or was maimed from birth, then this was a sure sign that an ancestor's sins were visited on the child. Even today this wrong concept is present in many a Christian believer. In such a situation let us ask the Holy Spirit to lead us into all truth so that we may live lives that are free from superstition and the bondage of fear.

In Jesus' time also people questioned Jesus about this. We read:

As Jesus walked along, he saw a man blind from birth. His disciples asked him, "Rabbi, who sinned, this man or his parents, that he was born blind?" Jesus answered, "Neither this man nor his parents sinned; he was born blind so that God's works might be revealed in him. We must work the works of him who sent me while it is day; night is coming when no one can work. As long as I am in the world, I am the light of the world" (Jn 9:1-5).

Jesus is the light of the world, as long as Jesus is with us we are in the light, that means that we are not deprived of the truth.

Then Jesus said to the blind man, "Go, wash in the pool of Siloam (which means Sent)" (Jn 9:7). Jesus is the one who was sent by the Father to bring the light of salvation to us. Hence, when we approach Jesus and allow him to cleanse us, all darkness (blindness is a symbol of darkness) will disappear, and we will see clearly.

Jesus Christ is the same yesterday, today and forever (Heb 13:8). Therefore, the person who sins, whatever be the time of history he/she has lived in, including the present time, is responsible for his/her own sins and will have to answer for them to the Lord if he/she does not repent.

Another passage from the Good News of Luke makes this point clearer: As Jesus taught his disciples and the crowds,

There were some present who told him about the Galileans whose blood Pilate had mingled with their sacrifices. Jesus asked them, "Do you think that because these Galileans suffered in this way they were worse sinners than all other Galileans? No, I tell you; but unless you repent, you will all perish as they did. Or those eighteen who were killed when the tower of Siloam fell on them, do you think that they were worse offenders than all the others living in Jerusalem? No, I tell you; but unless you repent, you will all perish just as they did" (Lk 13:1-5).

Thus, instead of pointing to others' sins as being responsible for our sufferings, let us look into our own hearts and see how we have been the cause of suffering for ourselves and for others, and without any delay or hesitation let us repent for our wrongdoings.

In our world of today, the values of the Gospel of Jesus Christ seem less evident, and the sense of sin and repentance seems to diminish day by day. We are living in a highly permissive society where every strange and sinful behavior is becoming the fashion of the day. But let us not become discouraged, remembering what Jesus said: "We must work the works of him who sent me, while it is day; night comes, when no one can work" (Jn 9:4).

Although this age may be like the night when no one can work the holy works of God, we cannot lose heart because Jesus immediately adds: "As long as I am in the world, I am the light of the world!" (Jn 9:5). And we know and believe that Jesus is alive among us today by the power of his Holy Spirit, his word, and the sacraments.

Hence, we, the members of the body of Christ, the Church, have the responsibility of keeping the light of the risen Lord Jesus burning bright in and through our lives of faithful service to God and his people, so that the works of darkness may not prevail.

Now to him who by the power at work within us is able to accomplish abundantly far more than all we can ask or imagine, to him be glory in the church and in Christ Jesus to all generations, forever and ever. Amen (Eph 3:20-21).

EZEKIEL 34:2-16, 23-24

*Thus says the Lord GOD: Ho, shepherds . . . who have been feeding your-
selves! Should not shepherds feed the sheep? You eat the fat, you clothe
yourselves with the wool, you slaughter the fatlings; but you do not
feed the sheep . . . The weak you have not strengthened, the sick you
have not healed, the crippled you have not bound up, the strayed you
have not brought back, the lost you have not sought . . . So they were
scattered, because there was no shepherd . . . I myself will search for
my sheep, and will seek them out . . . I will feed them with good pas-
ture . . . I myself will be the shepherd of my sheep, and I will make them
lie down, says the Lord GOD. I will seek the lost, and I will bring back
the strayed, and I will bind up the crippled, and I will strengthen the
weak . . . I will set up over them one shepherd, my servant David, and
he shall feed them: he shall feed them and be their shepherd. And I, the
LORD, will be their God, and my servant David shall be prince among
them; I, the LORD, have spoken.*

King David lived centuries before the time that the prophet
Ezekiel spoke these words of prophecy. Hence, the title "my servant David" refers to the coming Messiah (the anointed one) who
would descend from David's line and be the good shepherd promised by God.

The angel Gabriel announced to the Virgin Mary of Nazareth,
saying,

*You will conceive in your womb and bear a son, and you will
name him Jesus . . . and the Lord God will give to him the throne
of his ancestor David. He will reign over the house of Jacob forever, and of his kingdom there will be no end (Lk 1:31-33).*

God says to the leaders of the people, "Should not the shepherds feed the sheep? . . . but you do not feed the sheep . . . the sick
you have not healed, the crippled you have not bound up, the

strayed you have not brought back, the lost you have not sought . . . So they were scattered, because there was no shepherd."

Jesus says to the leaders and to the people, "I came that they may have life, and have it abundantly. I am the good shepherd" (Jn 10:10-11). All that Ezekiel said that the shepherds had not done for the sheep, we see that Jesus has done for all those who came to him. Jesus went about all the cities and villages, teaching and proclaiming the good news of the kingdom. He cured every disease and sickness. The evangelists tell us, "When he saw the crowds, he had compassion for them, because they were harassed and helpless, like sheep without a shepherd" (Mt 9:36).

When the apostles returned from their first missionary experience, Jesus took them away to a quiet deserted place so that they could rest there and share their experiences without being disturbed by the crowds who usually left them with no leisure even to eat. So they went away by themselves in the boat to a deserted place. However, many people saw them and followed them.

> As Jesus went ashore, he saw a great crowd; and he had compassion for them, because they were like sheep without a shepherd; and he began to teach them many things (Mk 6:34, emphasis added).

Jesus, the good shepherd, knew that the deepest need of the people was to have knowledge of God and his holy will. So the first thing he did was to teach the crowds. The prophet Jeremiah had foretold this: "I will give you shepherds after my own heart, who will feed you with knowledge and understanding" (Jer 3:15).

Jesus was the shepherd after God's own heart who knew the right diet for the people and who fed them holistically, as it were, first with the spiritual food of God's word and then also with physical food of bread and fish. For example, Jesus was teaching them many things, and:

When it grew late, his disciples came to him and said, "This is a deserted place, and the hour is now very late; send them away so that they may go into the surrounding country and villages and buy something for themselves to eat." But he answered them, "You give them something to eat."... Then he ordered them to get all the people to sit down in groups on the green grass... Taking the five loaves and the two fish, Jesus looked up to heaven, and blessed and broke the loaves, and gave them to his disciples to set before the people; and he divided the two fish among them all. And all ate and were filled (Mk 6:35-44).

The shepherds had the responsibility of not only feeding the sheep but also of binding up their wounds and healing them. When any sheep strayed away and got lost, the shepherd was to go and search for it, as we read in the text from Ezekiel. But many leaders of the people had not done any of these works of compassion for the sheep. Rather, they had fed on the sheep and enjoyed all the benefits that came from the sheep. Therefore, God said: "I myself will be their shepherd."

In the person of Jesus, God became the shepherd of his people. Jesus said,

I am the good shepherd. The good shepherd lays down his life for the sheep. He who is a hireling and not a shepherd... sees the wolf coming and leaves the sheep and flees... I am the good shepherd, I know my own and my own know me... I lay down my life for the sheep (Jn 10:7-14).

Jesus is the good shepherd who feeds us and binds up our wounds. He heals the sick and broken-hearted. He goes in search of the lost and rejoices when he has found them. We learn about Jesus from all that he said and did, but especially from his parables.

When Jesus taught the crowds and disciples, even the Pharisees and the scribes came to listen to him so that they could find fault with him. It happened that,

> *All the tax-collectors and sinners were coming near to listen to Jesus. And the Pharisees and the scribes were grumbling and saying, "This man welcomes sinners and eats with them." So Jesus told them this parable: "Which one of you, having a hundred sheep and losing one of them, does not leave the ninety-nine in the wilderness and go after the one that is lost until he finds it? When he has found it, he lays it on his shoulders and rejoices. And when he comes home, he calls together his friends and neighbors, saying to them, 'Rejoice with me, for I have found my sheep that was lost.' Just so, I tell you, there will be more joy in heaven over one sinner who repents than over ninety-nine righteous persons who need no repentance"* (Lk 15:1-7).

Jesus tells this parable starting with a question: "which one of you . . .?" Of course, the usual answer was that no one would be so foolish to leave ninety-nine in the wilderness by themselves, to go after one lost sheep.

But this, precisely, is the difference between Jesus, the Good Shepherd, and other shepherds. Jesus seeks the lost and celebrates with rejoicing when he has found even one. Jesus goes through much suffering and shame and even death on a cross just because he wants to save the lost and bring them back to the Father. Jesus lays down his life for his sheep, and he takes it up again in the resurrection so that we too might rise from the dead and live with him forever.

The Prophet Daniel

DANIEL 7:13-14

I saw in the night visions, and behold, with the clouds of heaven there came one like a son of man; and he came to the Ancient of Days and was presented before him. And to him was given dominion and glory and kingdom, that all peoples, nations and languages should serve him; his dominion is an everlasting dominion, which shall not pass away, and his kingdom one that shall not be destroyed.

The angel Gabriel had promised Mary that the son she would bear would be great and "the Lord God will give to him the throne of his ancestor David. He will reign over the house of Jacob forever, and of his kingdom, there will be no end" (Lk 1:32-33).

In the prophetic vision of Daniel we see all glory and everlasting dominion being given to the son of man who stood before God the Creator and Master of all ages.

Whenever Jesus spoke of himself he would use the title, the Son of Man. Indeed, all that had been prophesied in Daniel about the Son of Man was experienced in the life, words, and works of Jesus. After accomplishing the saving work that God had sent him into the world for, Jesus ascended to the Father and all dominion and glory were given to him forever.

God put this power to work in Christ when he raised him from the dead and seated him at his right hand in the heavenly places, far above all rule and authority and power and domin- ion, and above every name that is named, not only in this age but also in the age to come. And he has put all things under his feet and has made him the head over all things (Eph 1:20-23).

For the Son of Man is to come with his angels in the glory of his Father, and then he will repay everyone for what has been done (Mt 16:27).

Even though Jesus Christ had in himself all power and glory, we know that he emptied himself of all glory from the moment he was born of the Virgin Mary and laid in a manger, "because there was no place for them in the inn" (Lk 1:7). Jesus never doubted his exalted identity and the responsibility that went with it. He did not encourage fanfare and sensational gains at the cost of his power; rather, he discouraged such suggestions and thoughts at the very outset. For example, once a scribe came to Jesus and volun- teered to be his disciple. He said to Jesus,

"Teacher, I will follow you wherever you go." And Jesus said to him, "Foxes have holes, and birds of the air their nests; but the Son of Man has nowhere to lay his head" (Mt 8:19-20).

This is just one of the many instances where Jesus wanted to make clear that his disciples were to live as their Master did, not for worldly fame and gain, but for the glory that would be theirs in the eternal kingdom of God. Hence, their goal could not be this world and its gains. This would be too limited a sphere for their eternal vocation and mission. The cost of discipleship is nothing short of the daily carrying of the cross in every disciple's life (Lk 9:23), but this is always accompanied by the promise of inheriting all that belongs to Jesus in the Father's kingdom.

However, Jesus did not suppress or ignore his inner power when it came to giving life to those who came to him. Once, a paralyzed man was brought to Jesus by his friends, and Jesus, knowing the deeper need of the sick man, forgave him his sins first. But this made the scribes angry. The scribes were doctors of the law and they prided themselves for their knowledge of God and the law of Moses. Yet, they did not say anything aloud against Jesus but criticized him in their hearts. They said to themselves,

> "This man is blaspheming." But Jesus, knowing their thoughts, said, "Why do you think evil in your hearts? For which is easier, to say, 'Your sins are forgiven,' or to say, 'Rise and walk'? But that you may know that the Son of man has authority on earth to forgive sins" — he then said to the paralytic — "Rise, take up your bed and go home." And he rose and went home. When the crowds saw it, they were afraid, and they glorified God (Mt 9:3-8).

Besides the scribes, we can also see the Pharisees following Jesus around to find fault with his teachings and his works. Every sabbath, Jesus used to go to the synagogue and teach. His teachings were often accompanied by healings and miracles for those who needed to be touched by him. But this angered the Pharisees a great deal because they knew in their hearts that only God could do and say the things that Jesus said and did (cf. Mk 3:1-6). They refused to believe in him. They even tried to discourage the disciples from following Jesus. Their usual objection to the disciples was, "Why are they doing what is not lawful on the sabbath?" (Mk 2:24). Jesus explained why he did works of mercy and compassion on the sabbath. He emphasized that:

> The sabbath was made for man, not man for the sabbath; so the Son of Man is lord even of the sabbath (Mk 2:27-28).

Jesus revealed himself to his disciples in a special way. There were some details about himself that he would give only to them. After Peter made a declaration of faith in Jesus the Messiah (cf. Mk 8:27-29), Jesus began to teach them about the things that he was going to endure in the coming days, to fulfill all that the Messiah had to do to save humankind from sin and eternal death.

> *Jesus and his disciples went on from there and passed through Galilee. He did not want anyone to know it; for he was teaching his disciples, saying to them, "the Son of Man is to be betrayed into the hands of men, and they will kill him, and three days after being killed, he will rise again" (Mk 9:30-31).*

And Jesus promised his apostles, saying,

> *Truly I tell you, at the renewal of all things, when the Son of Man is seated on the throne of his glory, you who have followed me will also sit on twelve thrones, judging (Mt 19:28).*

When Jesus was on trial before the Council comprised of the scribes, the chief priests, and elders, the high priest Caiaphas said to him,

> *"I adjure you by the living God, tell us if you are the Christ, the Son of God." Jesus said to him, "You have said so. But I tell you, hereafter you will see the Son of man seated at the right hand of Power, and coming on the clouds of heaven." Then the high priest tore his robes, and said, "He has uttered blasphemy." (Mt 26:63-65).*

This was one moment when Jesus made it so clear that he truly was the Son of Man about whom the prophet Daniel had spoken. The council heard it and understood the fact, but refused to believe in Jesus. The high priest understood what Jesus was saying, but his heart remained stubborn. For him, Jesus was someone to be despised and done away with. He tore his clothes, a sign to declare that Jesus had blasphemed by claiming equality with God, and thus deserved death.

The Son of Man was with them and they did not accept him. Yet there were times when people would look for the Messiah and await his coming, just as the deer panting for running waters. Jesus knew this, and warned his disciples about false prophets, who would come and mislead them by claiming that they had the words of knowledge about the coming of the Son of Man. Hence,

Jesus said to the disciples, "The days are coming when you will long to see one of the days of the Son of Man, and you will not see it. They will say to you, 'Look there!' or 'Look here!' Do not go, do not set off in pursuit. For as the lightning flashes and lights up the sky from one side to the other, so will the Son of Man be in his day. But first he must endure much suffering and be rejected by this generation" (Lk 17:22-25).

Jesus taught clearly that when the Son of Man comes again to judge the living and the dead, no one will need to be told about his coming, because just as lightning in the sky is recognized by all who see it, so will the Son of Man be recognized by all at the same time when he comes. All we need to be equipped with in that Day is unfailing faith in Jesus. For Jesus himself asked, "And yet, when the Son of Man comes, will he find faith on earth?" (Lk 18:8).

Even though we read that there will be terrible signs and distress, and people will faint from fear, and so on, before the Son of Man comes again, yet Jesus sets our hearts at rest with his words:

Now when these things begin to take place, stand up and raise your heads, because your redemption is drawing near (Lk 21:28).

As we live our daily lives in this world, we are called to give witness to Jesus Christ by our words and godly living. Therefore, let us give up laziness and complacency and put on the armor of God (cf. Eph 6:11-20). In this world, there are many temptations to make our faith lukewarm and lead us to a cowardly compromise with the ideologies of this world. But just as Jesus never allowed the world to dictate its values and mediocrity to him, we too need not be taken in by the attractions of this world and its permissiveness. St. Peter says,

> Do not be intimidated, but in your hearts sanctify Christ as Lord. Always be ready to make your defense to anyone who demands from you an accounting for the hope that is in you (1 Pet 3:14b-15).

And Jesus promises, saying,

> I tell you, everyone who acknowledges me before others, the Son of Man also will acknowledge before the angels of God; but whoever denies me before others will be denied before the angels of God (Lk 12:8-9).

We can acknowledge Jesus before others in our day-to-day lives, as we live in imitation of Christ. Therefore, let us ask the Lord for the grace that we may be faithful to him and to all that he asks of us each day. May we never tire of doing what is right and just, and always be aware of the purpose for which God has called us in our new life in the Spirit.

Lord, Let the Son of Man, the Lord Jesus Christ, reign in our hearts today and always! Amen.

The Prophet Hosea

HOSEA 4:1b-2; 6:6

There is no faithfulness or loyalty, and no knowledge of God in the land. Swearing, lying and murder, and stealing and adultery break out; bloodshed follows bloodshed . . . I desire steadfast love and not sacrifice, the knowledge of God rather than burnt offerings.

God wants us to know him, and more than any prophet, it is Jesus who brings the true knowledge of God to us. Knowledge of God, according to the Bible, is always something *experiential*, and Jesus alone can bring this to us. Jesus, the faithful Servant of God, brings us the Father's love, and teaches us to be loyal and faithful to our God by keeping his commandments. Jesus also forgives us our sins and teaches us to forgive one another in our turn. He shows us that the Father is merciful, and he wants us to become like him. Jesus illustrates at great length how we can become like the Father (cf. Lk 6:20-49). And he says, "Be merciful, just as your Father is merciful" (Lk 6:36).

The prophet Hosea points out that the people were committing all kinds of sins because they had "no knowledge of God." God desires that his people attain knowledge of God and stop accumulating sin offerings and sacrifices. The prophet Jeremiah had also lamented that even the leaders of the people, namely, the priests and the "official" prophets, lived and behaved like those with no knowledge of God: "Both prophet and priest ply their trade throughout the land, and have no knowledge" (Jer 14:18b). These leaders had become self-centered and did whatever they wished, they did not care for God's commandments.

Already from early times, in order to give his people knowledge of himself, God gave them the law through Moses. The people's sinful behavior and selfish choices demonstrated clearly that they did not know the difference between what was God's will and what was not his will. They could not differentiate between good and evil. Therefore, God in his great mercy gave the law to teach his people how they were to conduct themselves as people belonging to the Lord.

They were to honor God's presence, worship him, and grow in intimacy with him. In order to grow in their relationship with God, they were to repent and give up their old habits of sin and live according to his commandments.

The law was meant to bring knowledge of God and his will. The role of the law was to point out what was sin, so that the sinner might repent and turn to the Lord. Hence, the law was good. It was a gift of God, but its purpose was temporary, to bring God's people back to him and keep them in his ways.

Once Jesus came and lived among us, and especially after his death and resurrection, when the new law of the Spirit was given, the old law was substituted. St. Paul explains:

> *If it had not been for the law, I would not have known sin. I would not have known what it is to covet if the law had not said, "You shall not covet." Apart from the law sin lies dead . . . So the law is holy, and commandment is holy and just and good . . . But now we are discharged from the law . . . so that we are servants not under the old written code but in the new life of the Spirit (Rom 7:7-12, 6).*

Jesus is the new Moses who teaches the people. Jesus did not do away with the law, but fulfilled it by his life, death and resurrection. To those who thought that Jesus' life and works had nothing to do with the law, Jesus said clearly,

Do not think that I have come to abolish the law or the prophets; I have come not to abolish but to fulfill . . . not one stroke of the letter will pass from the law until all is accomplished (Mt 5:17-19).

And Jesus accomplished all that was said in the law and the prophets. He kept God's law with all its commandments, and at the same time, he led the way beyond the old law to the perfect law of the Spirit:

The law of the Spirit of life in Christ Jesus has set you free from the law of sin and of death. For God has done what the law, weakened by the flesh, could not do: by sending his own Son in the likeness of sinful flesh, and to deal with sin, he condemned sin in the flesh, so that the just requirement of the law might be fulfilled in us, who walk not according to the flesh but according to the Spirit (Rom 8:2-4).

Jesus reveals the Father to all those who come to him with faith and love. Jesus rejoices that the Father chooses to reveal himself to those who are weak and foolish in the eyes of the world, but acceptable to God, for God does not judge by worldly standards. Jesus says,

All things have been handed over to me by my Father, and no one knows the Father except the Son and anyone to whom the Son chooses to reveal him (Mt 11:27).

Oh, how wonderful it would be if all of us, dear readers, would open ourselves to the knowledge of God coming through Jesus

Christ in the Holy Spirit! Then, through us, the whole world also can receive the true knowledge of God and turn to Him and live. This is also the hope of the prophet Habakkuk who looked forward to the time when, "The earth will be filled with the knowledge of the glory of the LORD, as the waters cover the sea" (Hab 2:14).

The Prophet Joel

JOEL 2:12-13

Yet even now, says the LORD, return to me with all your heart, with fasting, with weeping, and with mourning; rend your hearts and not your clothing. Return to the LORD, your God, for he is gracious and merciful, slow to anger, and abounding in steadfast love.

(1) "Return to the LORD, your God, for he is gracious and merciful, slow to anger, and abounding in steadfast love." The prophet calls the people to conversion. In their sinfulness and stubbornness, they have turned their backs and gone away from the Lord. We can all testify from our own experience that when we have behaved sinfully, it is quite difficult to return to the one whom we have sinned against. We are ashamed. We are upset. If we can, we would try to get out of the situation by justifying ourselves and putting the blame on someone else. We would even run away from the scene in order to escape humiliation. We are also afraid of the consequences.

However, we need not be afraid of returning to our God with a humble and contrite heart. Our God is gracious and merciful. His heart melts at the very first step we take of sincere repentance. Recall the parable Jesus told about the prodigal son who had left his father and family in pursuit of selfish pleasures. When all his riches were over, his "friends for a season" left him and he was miserable. He began to starve because no one gave him even animals' fodder to eat. His hunger reminded him of the abundance in his father's house. He decided to return to the father, and ask him to accept him as a servant, and not as a son anymore. But the father was gracious and merciful. He received his wayward son with great love and celebrated his return (Lk 15:11-24).

This is the motive for repentance, not that we would be accepted in a half-hearted way, but that we would be given back our full dignity and joy. God, who is rich in mercy, does this for us. The Lord says through the prophet Isaiah:

> Thus says the LORD: "Heaven is my throne and the earth my footstool; what is the house which you would build for me, and what is the place of my rest? All these things my hand has made, and so all these things are mine," says the LORD. "But this is the person to whom I look, the one who is humble and contrite in spirit, and trembles at my word" (Is 66:1-2).

Jesus looked into people's hearts and brought freedom from sin and deliverance from evil to all those who came to him. In fact, Jesus celebrated their new life and sat at table with them. Sinners, both men and women, were attracted to Jesus and were not afraid to come to him in their shame. They knew that he would forgive them and give them the grace to live a new life. The Pharisees and the scribes murmured against Jesus when sinners came to him. They said, "This man welcomes sinners and eats with them" (Lk 15:1).

Jesus knew what the leaders of the people thought of him, and how they were criticizing him. But this did not deter him from doing the Father's will. He explained, "Those who are well have no need of a physician, but those who are sick. Go and learn what this means, 'I desire mercy, not sacrifice.' For I have come to call not the righteous but sinners to repentance" (Mt 9:12-13; Lk 5:31).

We too can return to the Lord our Savior today: "O that today you would listen to his voice! Do not harden your hearts" (Ps 95:7b-8a).

The Lord is slow to anger and abounding in steadfast love. The beautiful thing about the love of Jesus is that we do not have to become pure and perfect before we can come to him. He makes us pure and holy once we have returned to him. Hence, we do not need to worry about how imperfect we are or how many sins we have accumulated. Nor should we allow fear to keep us away from him, because Jesus, who is perfect love, casts out all fear (cf. 1 Jn 4:18).

The sooner we come to the healing sacrament of his forgiveness, the sacrament of reconciliation, the better it will be for us, because then the allure of the world and the flesh will not be able to take us far away from our God. This sacrament is called a healing sacrament. Once we have received forgiveness and healing through the sacrament of reconciliation, we too can forgive and heal others by our forgiveness (cf. Mt 6:14-15).

No one can give to another what one does not oneself possess. Hence, we can forgive only when we have received forgiveness ourselves. By his forgiveness, Jesus gives us a heart of flesh so that we too can reach out to others. St. Paul says,

Blessed be the God and Father of our Lord Jesus Christ, the Father of mercies and God of all comfort, who comforts us in all our affliction, so that we may be able to comfort those who are in any way afflicted, with the comfort with which we ourselves are comforted by God (2 Cor 1:3-4).

(2) Jesus comforts us in all our afflictions and makes us whole. In fact, he knows that without his help we would be utterly lost. The disciples of Jesus too needed him all the time and depended on Jesus for everything. But there came a time when Jesus told them that he would have to leave them and go back to the Father from whom he had come. The disciples were quite sad. Then Jesus comforted them with the promise of *another* Advocate, the Holy Spirit, who would come and dwell with them and live in them forever. Jesus told them that the Holy Spirit would bring to their

minds all that he, Jesus, had taught them. The Spirit would give them the grace to live and work as Jesus had commanded them to do (Jn 14:16, 26).

The prophet Joel had prophesied about this gift of the promised Spirit. He proclaimed God's message, saying,

> Then I will pour out my spirit on all flesh; your sons and your daughters shall prophesy, your old men shall dream dreams, and your young men shall see visions. Even on the male and female slaves, in those days, I will pour out my spirit (Joel 2:28-29).

The gift of the Holy Spirit is for all people, old and young, men and women, masters and slaves. The Spirit comes to remove all discrimination and barriers from the hearts of people and nations. All who receive the Spirit receive the knowledge of God and his holy will. Their hearts are joined in unity and harmony and set on fire with love for God and all peoples, and they begin to speak the language of justice, truth and wisdom, and become witnesses of the Lord Jesus wherever they are.

When the Father and the Son poured out their Gift on Pentecost, the Holy Spirit descended upon the community of disciples, who were waiting in faith and in prayer. The Spirit came with the sound of a mighty wind and appeared as flames of fire resting upon them. We read:

> And there appeared to them tongues as of fire, distributed and resting on each one of them. And they were all filled with the Holy Spirit and began to speak in other tongues, as the Spirit gave them utterance (Acts 2:3-4).

The Spirit came as fire and rested on each of them. The image of the fire on that day was gentle and yet powerful. It did not come to destroy but to build a new community, a new order in the world.

And the leaders of the new order were to be the apostles and the disciples of Jesus. Down the ages since then, we have experienced this power in and through the Church and its leaders.

The same Spirit was shared among them equally, both the men and the women (Mother Mary was with them too, cf. Acts 1:14). They received the Gift and began speaking in tongues, which was heard and understood by outsiders in their own languages. Those who received this great sign from God in faith even understood what the disciples were saying. They were testifying to God's great deeds of power accomplished in Jesus Christ. Others, who were not open to the Spirit, made fun of the apostles, saying that they were drunk so early in the morning (9 A.M., cf. Acts 2:15). Let us look at the passage:

> Now there were devout Jews from every nation under heaven living in Jerusalem. And at this sound the crowd gathered and was bewildered, because each one heard them speaking in the native language of each. Amazed and astonished, they asked, "Are not all these speaking Galileans? And how is it that we hear, each of us, in our own native language? . . . In our own languages we hear them speaking about God's deeds of power." All were amazed and perplexed, saying to one another, "What does this mean?" But others sneered and said, "They are filled with new wine" (Acts 2:5-13).

Thus God fulfilled his promise and sent his Spirit upon all flesh. Jesus too kept his word and sent the Advocate, the Counselor, to all those who thirsted for him. Today Jesus is sending his Spirit upon you and me, are we thirsty for the Spirit?

The Spirit is given to us in a special way in our Baptism and Confirmation, thus marking us with the seal of the Father, the Son and the Holy Spirit. The Spirit comes to us in every sacrament that we receive. And not only in the sacraments, but he comes to us whenever we empty ourselves of all sin and evil and turn to him for an infilling of the Spirit. The Spirit makes us like Jesus, if we allow him to lead us and guide us. Jesus said,

> *I still have many things to say to you, but you cannot bear them now. When the Spirit of truth comes, he will guide you into all truth; for he will not speak on his own, but will speak whatever he hears, and he will declare to you the things that are to come. He will glorify me, because he will take what is mine and declare it to you (Jn 16:12-14).*

Let us ask Jesus to fill us with the gift of the Spirit, so that we can be led by the Spirit and give glory to him by bearing the fruit of the Spirit in our lives:

> *The fruit of the Spirit is love, joy, peace, patience, kindness, generosity, faithfulness, gentleness, and self-control . . . If we live by the Spirit, let us also be guided by the Spirit (Gal 5:22-25).*

The Prophet Amos

AMOS 8:11-12

The time is surely coming, says the Lord GOD, when I will send a famine on the land; not a famine of bread, or a thirst for water, but of hearing the words of the LORD. They shall wander from sea to sea, and from north to east; they shall run to and fro, seeking the word of the LORD, but they shall not find it.

As we continue seeking the face of Jesus in the texts of the Old Testament, we remember how day and night the people would gather around Jesus to hear the word of God. Even when Jesus wanted to be with his disciples alone, so that they could have some quiet time together after a hectic time of ministry, the people would not leave them alone but followed Jesus to every place. Mark tells us,

> *The apostles gathered around Jesus, and told him all that they had done and taught. He said to them, "Come away to a deserted place all by yourselves and rest a while." For many were coming and going, and they has no leisure even to eat. And they went away in a boat to a deserted place by themselves. Now many saw them going and recognized them, and they hurried there on foot from all the towns and arrived ahead of*

them. As he went ashore, he saw a great crowd; and he had compassion for them, because they were like sheep without a shepherd; and he began to teach them many things (Mk 6:30-34, emphasis added).

Notice, Jesus wanted to be alone with his apostles. But the crowds did not allow him to do so. Yet, he did not get irritated with them or send them away. Rather, Jesus had compassion on them because they were like sheep without a shepherd. And knowing their deepest need to know God and his ways, Jesus began to teach them many things.

Jesus fed them with his word. He knew that whatever he taught them would light up their lives and they would gain wisdom of heart. Hence, he spoke to them about many things and at great length. And they hung on his words.

However, not all his listeners were ready to receive his words in faith. His teachings were not always easy to understand, faith was essential in order to accept Jesus' words. Hence, even many of his disciples had difficulty in accepting Jesus' teaching about his body and blood, and they grumbled, "This teaching is difficult; who can accept it?" But Jesus knowing that some of his disciples were complaining about his teaching, said to them,

The words that I have spoken to you are spirit and life. But among you there are some who do not believe (Jn 6:60-64).

The apostles listened to Jesus' words and accepted them. When many of his disciples no longer followed Jesus, he turned to the twelve apostles and asked them, "Do you also wish to go away?" Then Peter answered on behalf of all the apostles, saying,

Lord, to whom can we go? You have the words of eternal life. We have come to believe and know that you are the Holy One of God (Jn 6:68-69).

Jesus is indeed the Holy One of God. He is the Word of God himself. St. John begins his Good News with these words,

In the beginning was the Word, and the Word was with God, and the Word was God. All things came into being through him ... And the Word became flesh and lived among us, and we have seen his glory (Jn 1:1-3, 14).

The glory of the Lord could only be seen by those who had faith in Jesus and his words. There were even people who believed that Jesus' words had power without his being physically present. Take for example the centurion whose servant was lying at home paralyzed and in great distress. He came to Jesus and told him about his servant, and Jesus said to him, "'I will come and heal him.' But the centurion answered him, 'Lord, I am not worthy to have you come under my roof; but only say the word, and my servant will be healed'" (Mt 5:7-8). And Jesus praised the centurion's faith before all the people, "and to the centurion Jesus said, 'Go; be it done for you as you have believed.' And the servant was healed at that very moment" (Mt 8:13).

Jesus came to give us life abundantly, and his word was the rich source of nourishment and knowledge of the truth, so that no one would live in darkness any more but follow the light of life. If we did not have his teachings, there would be only misery, famine, and the bondage of ignorance. The words that God spoke through the prophet Amos present such a sad and shocking image:

I will send a famine on the land; not a famine of bread ... but of hearing the words of the LORD ... they shall run to and fro, to seek the word of the LORD, but they shall not find it (Amos 8:11-12).

When two close friends have some sad misunderstanding among themselves, and one of them says to the other, "I will not speak with you ever again," imagine how painful it is for the other friend. Surely, this friend would do everything to make things right between them so that the silence would be ended, and they could once again enjoy each other's company, and talk and share their thoughts and experiences with one another as before.

It is a fact that we cannot share everything with everyone. But with a trusted friend we can share all the secrets of our hearts. And our God has shared all his secrets with us in Jesus Christ.

The Father has spoken through his Son, Jesus Christ, our Lord and Savior. Jesus faithfully shares with us everything that the Father told him. And he wants this communication to continue, so that we too can hear and speak his words to all who want to hear God's word. Jesus said,

> *I do not call you servants any longer, because the servant does not know what the master is doing; but I have called you friends, because I have made known to you everything that I have heard from my Father (Jn 15:15).*

When Jesus was preparing to go back to the Father, he promised to send the Holy Spirit who would continue the communication between God and us. We too need to keep our hearts open in obedience to God's will for us, otherwise, we may wander away into sinful, dark paths and get lost in the maze of this world's noise and attractions. Then we will lose the life-giving word of the Lord and end up dying of starvation, because it is true that we cannot live on bread alone but need the spiritual nourishment that comes from every word that proceeds from the mouth of the Lord (cf. Deut 8:3; Mt 4:4).

The Prophet Jonah

JONAH 3:3-5; 1:17; 2:10

So Jonah set out and went to Nineveh . . . a three days' walk across. Jonah began to go into the city, going a day's walk. And he cried out, "Forty days more, and Nineveh shall be overthrown!" . . . And the people of Nineveh believed God; they proclaimed a fast, and everyone, great and small, put on sackcloth.

If there was ever a disobedient prophet, it was the one we find in the book of Jonah. In the whole book of Jonah we can see how every one, humans and animals included, obeyed God, but his own prophet was busy running away from the mission that God was trying to give him. In the end, however, he had to stop running away, because no one can run and hide from the Lord.

The author tells us that very reluctantly the prophet went and announced the message of repentance to the enemies of Israel, the Ninevites. And the response of Nineveh, of the rulers, the people and the animals, was immediate and positive. They all repented and begged God for mercy. This was precisely what Jonah did not want because he hated the Ninevites and wanted to see them destroyed. In fact, when they repented the Lord God forgave them and did not punish them.

There are two important points in this whole story of Jonah that Jesus speaks about:

(1) When the scribes and the Pharisees and the crowds pressed Jesus for signs and wonders, Jesus said that the only sign that would be given to them would be the sign of Jonah.

> *When the crowds were increasing, he began to say, "This gen-eration is an evil generation; it asks for a sign, but no sign will be given to it except the sign of Jonah. For just as Jonah became a sign to the people of Nineveh, so the Son of Man will be to this generation . . . The people of Nineveh will rise up at the judgment with this generation and condemn it, because they repented at the proclamation of Jonah, and see, something greater than Jonah is here!" (Lk 11:29-32; cf. Mt 16:4)*

Jesus says, just as Jonah became a sign to the people of Nin-eveh, so the Son of Man will be to this generation. The preaching of Jonah made the people of Nineveh repent of their sins and turn from the evils they had committed. The preaching of Jesus should have been even more fruitful, for after John the Baptist was arrested, Jesus came to the region of Galilee where he had grown up, and he preached the good news of God, proclaiming, "The time is fulfilled, and the kingdom of God is at hand; repent, and believe in the good news" (Mk 1:15).

And through many teachings, exhortations and works, Jesus explained what he meant by saying that the time was fulfilled, the kingdom of God was at hand, and how they were to repent and believe in the good news.

But, as we have seen, many of those who followed Jesus only did so for the signs and wonders that he performed. They were not ready to listen to his words and obey them. Nor were they ready to believe that he had been sent by God. Hence, Jesus said that the people of Nineveh would rise up at the judgment with this generation and condemn it, because they repented at the proclamation of Jonah, while this generation was refusing to listen to someone greater than Jonah! Jesus is far greater than Jonah, and he is sent to his own people, but sadly, as St. John says, "He came to his own, and his own received him not" (Jn 1:11).

Let us take a look into our own hearts today, and ask ourselves: are we seeking the face of the Lord and listening to his words so that we can live according to his commands in our day to day lives? Or, are we only interested in the blessings of the Lord? The Lord does not look for perfect disciples; rather, he makes us perfect step by step as we follow his ways with sincere and generous hearts. Let us open our hearts to him and invite him to come in. He will surely come in and make something beautiful of our lives.

(2) Jesus took another incident from the story of Jonah and gave it as the sign for those who sought his signs and wonders. We read:

> The LORD provided a large fish to swallow up Jonah; and Jonah was in the belly of the fish three days and three nights... Then the LORD spoke to the fish, and it spewed Jonah out upon the dry land (Jon 1:17; 2:10).

As Jesus walked among the people and taught and healed them:

> Some of the scribes and Pharisees said to him, "Teacher, we wish to see a sign from you." But he answered them, "An evil and adulterous generation asks for a sign, but no sign will be given to it except the sign of the prophet Jonah. For just as Jonah was three days and three nights in the belly of the sea monster, so for three days and three nights the Son of Man will be in the heart of the earth" (Mt 12:38-40).

With this sign of Jonah, Jesus clearly pointed to his death, burial, and resurrection as the definitive sign of his divine sonship and authority. This sign would require faith in the hearts of his listeners, because these events would take place in the future. This sign of the resurrection would open the hearts and minds of the disciples to the reality of their Master Jesus Christ, and they would become his witnesses to the ends of the earth.

After Jesus died and was buried, he rose on the third day and appeared to the disciples. He moved among with them for forty days, after which he ascended into heaven, and together with the Father sent the Holy Spirit. The Spirit empowered them to proclaim the good news of Jesus Christ and live as a community of believers. Jesus had told them all these things before his death, and those who remained faithful to the words of Jesus through faith, and not by demanding visible proofs, have shared in the ministry of Jesus down the ages even to the present times.

Today, as we seek the face of Jesus through the sacred scriptures, let us once again believe all that Jesus said and did, for us and for our salvation. Then we too will experience a new Pentecost and the Holy Spirit will lead us into the light of Jesus' presence, to be empowered for the works that Jesus calls us to do in his name.

The Prophet Micah

MICAH 5:2-5

But you, O Bethlehem of Ephrathah, who are one of the little clans of Judah, from you shall come forth for me one who is to rule in Israel, whose origin is from of old, from ancient days . . . And he shall stand and feed his flock in the strength of the LORD, in the majesty of the name of the LORD his God . . . he shall be the one of peace.

(1) The prophet Micah tells us about the will of God concerning the birthplace of the Messiah. It is to be Bethlehem, the city of David, for the Messiah would be a descendant of David, as the angel confirmed later to Mary (cf. Lk 1:32). He would rule in Israel, but his origin would be from ancient days (cf. Jn 1:1-2, 14). The Messiah would be the good shepherd who would care for his sheep and lay down his life for them (Jn 10:14-15). He would be the Prince of Peace.

In the Good News according to Matthew and Luke, we see the newborn babe, wrapped in swaddling clothes, lying in a manger, with Mary and Joseph surrounding him with their love and warmth. There was no place for them in the inn in Bethlehem, and no place in the hearts of the leaders. Thus even before he was born, Jesus suffered rejection. When he was born, Jesus became a threat to the powers of this world.

When the wise men, who with open hearts, came from the eastern lands to Jerusalem, to ask Herod about where they should go to pay homage to the newborn king, they met only with cunning and envy. But because their hearts were right with God, God led them to the place where Jesus was born. We read:

> *In the time of King Herod, after Jesus was born . . . wise men from the East came to Jerusalem, asking, "Where is the child who has been born king of the Jews? For we observed his star at its rising, and have come to pay him homage." When King Herod heard this, he was frightened, and all Jerusalem with him; and calling together all the chief priests and scribes of the people, he inquired of them where the Messiah was to be born. They told him, "In Bethlehem of Judea; for so it has been written by the prophet . . ." Then Herod secretly called for the wise men and learned from them the exact time when the star had appeared. Then he sent them to Bethlehem, saying, "Go and search diligently . . . so that I may also go and pay him homage." . . . The star stopped over the place where the child was . . . they entered the place . . . knelt down and paid him homage . . . they offered him gifts of gold, frankincense, and myrrh. And having been warned in a dream not to return to Herod, they left for their own country by another road (Mt 2:1-12).*

The lovely face of the child Jesus brings great joy to us every time we celebrate Christmas. Let us pause for a moment here, and reflect on the face of the babe wrapped in swaddling clothes lying in a manger, with Mary and Joseph gazing upon him in tremendous love, joy, and contentment. All their tiredness and darkness of the surroundings where baby Jesus lay were transformed into joy and gladness as the face of Jesus shone before their eyes.

We can imagine the great joy of the wise men who came to acknowledge the greatness of Jesus and pay homage to him.

Even the shepherds who had heard the good news from heavenly messengers came in "haste and found Mary and Joseph, and the child lying in the manger... They returned, glorifying God for all they had heard and seen, as it had been told them" (Lk 2:16-20).

Jesus is good news to all those who believe in him, people both great and small (such as the wise men and the shepherds). We too can receive the good news of Jesus and be filled with new and abundant life, all we need is to seek him with faith in our hearts and accept him as our Saviour. Jesus came to give life and freedom and not to condemn anyone. Let us open our hearts and receive his message of salvation.

(2) The prophet Micah announces what true religion means:

He has told you what is good; and what does the LORD *require of you but to do justice, and to love kindness, and to walk humbly with your God? (Mic 6:8).*

"Do justice, love kindness, and walk humbly with your God." Jesus teaches these attitudes of a sincere believer in the Beatitudes which he taught during his Sermon on the Mount. Jesus said: "Blessed are the poor in spirit, for theirs is the kingdom of heaven" (Mt 5:3).

The people who are poor in spirit are the ones who walk humbly with their God. Let us look into our hearts and search whether we are poor in spirit. Jesus has a fundamental option for the poor, those who are poor materially, as well as those who may be rich materially but are spiritually lowly and humble. This means that they acknowledge the fact that whatever they have is God's gift to them, to be used also for the good of those who do not have any possessions.

The poor in spirit are those who rely daily on the Lord to take care of them. They do not rely on their own possessions, power, and accomplishments, independently of God. When they have what they need they do not set about accumulating or hoarding goods in order to secure their own future. Each day they live their lives according to the words of the Lord, who says,

> *I tell you, do not worry about your life, what you will eat or what you will drink, or about your body, what you will wear. Is not life more than food, and the body more than clothing? Look at the birds of the air; they neither sow nor reap nor gather into barns, and yet your heavenly Father feeds them. Are you not of more value than they? . . . indeed your heavenly Father knows that you need all these things. But strive first for the kingdom of God and his righteousness, and all these things will be given to you as well (Mt 6:25-33).*

Hence, those who walk humbly with their God are the poor in spirit, committed to doing the Lord's will day by day.

Those who love the Lord and do justice and love kindness are those of whom Jesus says,

> *Blessed are those who hunger and thirst for justice, for they will be filled . . . Blessed are the merciful, for they will receive mercy (Mt 5:6-7).*

The teachings of Jesus include a demand and a promise. The demand explains the cost of discipleship, and the promise gives hope in God's fidelity. Those who do justice and work for justice are also the ones who depend on God and not on themselves to bring about justice. And God does not disappoint them, for all their efforts bear good fruit and they themselves are satisfied.

Those who are kind to others will receive God's kindness. Those who have mercy in their hearts towards others will receive mercy from God. Jesus explains that those who have been merciful need not have any fear of judgment, because when the Lord comes in judgment he will bless those who have been merciful and generous towards others (Mt 25:34-40). Let us open our ears and hearts and listen to what Jesus says: "Be merciful, just as your Father is merciful" (Lk 6:36).

This is possible if we keep the Lord's words in our hearts and cherish them. Jesus teaches us that we are to love our enemies, to do good to those who hate us, to bless those who curse us, and to pray for those who abuse us (Lk 6:27ff). And Jesus also teaches us to forgive countless times and not to hold a grudge against anyone (cf. Mt 18:21-22).

Let us ask the Holy Spirit to fill us with the grace and the obedience we need to practice in our lives all that Jesus teaches us today and every day of our lives. Come Holy Spirit, purify our hearts and teach us to live lives pleasing to our God. Amen.

The Prophet Habakkuk

HABAKKUK 3:17-19

Though the fig tree does not blossom, and no fruit is on the vines; though the produce of the olive fails and the fields yield no food; though the flock is cut off from the fold and there is no herd in the stalls, yet I will rejoice in the LORD; I will exult in the God of my salvation.

The prophet Habakkuk lived and prophesied at a time when there was great distress in Judah. The land was under siege and was soon going to be destroyed. Habakkuk questioned the Lord because he could not accept that God's chosen people should have to suffer at the hands of foreign powers. He felt that these were more wicked than God's unfaithful people. He asked:

> *O LORD . . . why do you look on the treacherous, and are silent when the wicked swallow those more righteous than they? (Hab 1:13b).*

> *And the LORD answered him saying, "Look at the proud! Their spirit is not right in them, but the righteous live by their faith" (Hab 2:4, emphasis added).*

The Lord's answer to the prophet made clear that although the Lord purifies his people with suffering even at the hands of other nations, yet if they keep their faith and fidelity toward the Lord, then no suffering can vanquish them. They would have life because they believed in the Lord their God.

Jesus constantly called his disciples to believe and not to be afraid. He would say, "Why are you afraid, you of little faith?" (Mt 8:26).

Fear is the opposite of faith. Hence, when we give in to doubts and fears with regard to God's love and action on our behalf, it clearly shows up our weak faith. We have believed superficially if our faith does not hold up when we face trials.

"Faith is the assurance of things hoped for, the conviction of things not seen" (Heb 11:1). Faith therefore means, seeing, judging, and living the reality of life according to God's perspective. God sees all things and knows all things. When we see reality from God's perspective, then we are strengthened to believe, and have a confidence that goes beyond understanding.

Jesus believed in his Father's presence, love, and action in his own life and in the lives of his people, even unto the cross. Recall how Jesus felt abandoned on the cross and cried out to the Father, "My God, my God, why have you forsaken me?" (Mk 15:34). This did not mean that Jesus no longer believed in his Father, or that his faith had become weak. On the contrary, at the very next moment, Jesus entrusted himself totally and into the hands of the Father, saying, "Father, into your hands I commit my spirit" (Lk 23:46). By his own example Jesus teaches us what faith is.

The same conviction "of things not seen" is found in the life of Mother Mary, who believed even when all the promises of God seemed only a dream. Her walk with Jesus all through his earthly life, even unto his death, was done in faith. Everything in Mary, even her power of understanding, was subordinated to her faith. She received and experienced the divine mysteries within herself, not with intellectual understanding, but in faith. When Mother

Mary was faced with a mystery that went beyond her understanding, she would reflect on the words of Jesus, and on the events that she had taken part in, habitually preserving her memories and pondering them in her heart. We read:

And all who heard it were amazed at what the shepherds told them. But Mary treasured all these words and pondered them in her heart... Jesus said to them, "Why were you searching for me? Did you not know that I must be in my Father's house?" But they did not understand what he said to them... His mother treasured all these things in her heart (Lk 2:19, 51).

And because Mary was so contemplative during every moment of her pilgrimage, she could be greatly active in apostolic activity. In Mary, contemplation truly led to action! The story of Cana is a good example of this. Like Mary our faith too must lead to action, "for it is God who is at work in you, enabling you both to will and to work for his good pleasure" (Phil 2:13). Thus faith must be shown in good works in the footsteps of Christ Jesus our Lord.

Jesus praised those who believed in him even without seeing him physically. Jesus praises us who seek his face through the words of sacred scripture and believe in him at all times.

After Jesus rose from the dead he appeared to his disciples but Thomas was absent that day. He did not accept what the other disciples told him about the risen Lord. So some days later,

Although the doors were shut, Jesus came and stood among them and said, "Peace be with you." Then he said to Thomas, "Put your finger here and see my hands. Reach out your hand and put it in my side. Do not doubt but believe." Thomas answered, "My Lord and my God!" Jesus said to him, "Have you believed because you have seen me? Blessed are those who have not seen and yet have come to believe" (Jn 20:26-29).

These words of Jesus apply to us, because we believe in Jesus even without seeing and being with him, as the apostles could in their day. In times of trials and sorrows, let us not give up faith, but let us change these very experiences into opportunities to deepen our faith in the God who is love and compassion. For God, "will not let you be tested beyond your strength, but with the testing he will also provide the way out so that you may be able to endure it" (1 Cor 10:13).

Jesus encourages us today with his words of promise saying,

See, I am coming soon; my reward is with me, to repay according to everyone's work. I am the Alpha and the Omega, the first and the last, the beginning and the end (Rev 22:12-13).

Amen. Come, Lord Jesus!

The Prophet Zephaniah

ZEPHANIAH 3:14-17

*Sing aloud, O daughter Zion . . . Rejoice and exult with all your heart, O daughter Jerusalem! . . . The L*ORD*, your God, is in your midst . . . he will exult over you with loud singing as on a day of festival.*

As we read this joyful exhortation of the prophet Zephaniah addressing the people of God as the Daughter Zion in the immediate context of the prophet's times, we can also see in this address the beautiful face of the one person who personified the people of God in herself, as it emerges through the pages of the Bible. This is the Mother of Jesus and our Mother.

In the accounts of the Annunciation and the Visitation as presented by the evangelist Luke, we see that Mary is the Daughter of Zion (the Church teaches this in Vatican II's Dogmatic Constitution on The Church, *Lumen Gentium*, n. 55). Here, "daughter of Zion" is understood in the sense that this expression had in the Old Testament, that is, a personification of the People of God.

When the angel greeted Mary saying, "The Lord is with you!" (Lk 1:28), the greeting recalled the promises of the coming of the Messiah to his holy city (cf. Zeph 3:14 and 9:9). In the name of all the people of God, Mary received the annunciation of salvation. She gave her consent freely, and thus made its fulfillment possible.

I am reminded of the beautiful words of Hans Urs Von Balthasar (*The Glory of the Lord*, vol. I, Edinburgh: T. & T. Clark Ltd./San Francisco: Ignatius Press, 1982, p. 338), who described this important role of Mary when he wrote,

> At the point where all roads meet, which lead from the Old Testament to the New, we encounter the Marian experience of God, at once so rich and so secret that it almost escapes description. But it is also so important, that time and again it shines through as the background for what is manifest. In Mary, Zion passes over into the Church; the Word passes over into the flesh.

In Mary, the Old passes into the New Covenant, the Daughter of Zion becomes the Mother of the Messiah. Writing about Mary, the woman found "at the center of the salvific event," Pope John Paul II explains,

> It may be easy to think of the event (of the Annunciation) in the setting of the history of Israel, the Chosen People of which Mary is a daughter ... Mary attains a union with God that exceeds all the expectations of all Israel, in particular the daughters of this Chosen People, who, on the basis of the promise, could hope that one of their number would one day become the mother of the Messiah (Apostolic Letter, *Mulieris Dignitatem*, On the Dignity and Vocation of Women on the occasion of the Marian Year, 15 August, 1988, Vatican City: Polyglot Press, 1988, n. 3).

Truly, the whole existence and purpose of Mary's life are bound up with the Incarnation of the Savior, Jesus Christ. In her face we see the face of Jesus too, shining and radiant, through all the ages. Her face radiates his light, and its glow never fades. Let us together approach our Mother who will teach us the ways of the Lord in gentleness and faithfulness. She can bring joy and meaning into our lives so wrought with anxiety and confusion. Her light brings peace and love. With Elizabeth let us say,

> *Blessed are you among women, and blessed is the fruit of your womb . . . And blessed is she who believed that there would be a fulfillment of what was spoken to her by the Lord (Lk 1:42-45).*

The Prophet Zechariah

ZECHARIAH 9:9; 12:10

Rejoice greatly, O daughter Zion! Shout aloud, O daughter Jerusalem! Lo, your king comes to you; triumphant and victorious is he, humble and riding on a donkey, on a colt, the foal of a donkey.

(1) In these words of the prophet we can see the face of Jesus shining with determination to go to Jerusalem and complete the work for which the Father had sent him. Jesus did everything as was ordained by God. He could have entered walking into the city, but he humbled himself and kept the word of God spoken about the Messiah-king. Therefore, he sent his disciples into the village to bring a donkey and a colt tied with her, so that he could enter Jerusalem mounted on them.

> *The disciples went and did as Jesus had directed them; they brought the donkey and the colt, and put their cloaks on them, and he sat on them. A very large crowd spread their cloaks on the road, and others cut branches from the trees and spread them on the road. The crowds that went ahead of him and that followed were shouting, "Hosanna to the Son of David! Blessed is the one who comes in the name of the Lord! Hosanna in the highest heaven!" (Mt 21:1-9; cf. Jn 12:12-15).*

St. John tells us that "his disciples did not understand these things at first; but when Jesus was glorified, then they remembered that these things had been written of him and had been done to him" (Jn 12:16).

We too may not understand all that Jesus said and did, but that is less important. What is more important is our consent of faith to Jesus, who came to deliver us from sin and death. He came that we may have life in all its fullness. See, how beautifully Jesus did all things as the Father had willed and declared through the prophets centuries before Jesus was born. So open was Jesus to the Father's plan of salvation for our sake, that his response to the Father, even from the depths of his suffering was, "Lo, I have come to do your will" (Heb 10:7, 9).

(2) The prophet Zechariah proclaimed the word of the Lord concerning the mourning for the one who had been pierced:

> And I will pour out a spirit of compassion and supplication on the house of David and the inhabitants of Jerusalem, so that, when they look on the one whom they have pierced, they shall mourn for him, *as one mourns for an only child, and weep bitterly over him, as one weeps over a firstborn* (Zech 12:10, emphasis added).

The crucified Jesus bowed his head and gave up his spirit. Then we read:

> Since it was the day of Preparation, the Jews did not want the bodies left on the cross during the sabbath, especially because the sabbath was a day of great solemnity. So they asked Pilate to have the legs of the crucified men broken and the bodies removed. Then the soldiers came and broke the legs of the first and of the other who had been crucified with him. But when they came to Jesus and saw that he was already dead, they did

not break his legs. Instead, one of the soldiers pierced his side with a spear, and at once blood and water came out . . . These things occurred so that the scripture might be fulfilled, "None of his bones shall be broken." And again another passage of scripture says, "They will look on the one whom they have pierced" (Jn 19:31-37).

Jesus' side was pierced with a lance. And even today when we reflect on that brutality of the soldiers, the face of Jesus full of compassion rises before our eyes, and we can only bow down and worship Jesus our loving Savior.

In his loving wisdom, God works all things out for the good of those who love him and believe in him. Thus, from the pierced side of Jesus flowed blood and water, symbols of life. Blood and water are the components in the mother's womb by which her baby is formed.

The wisdom of the Fathers of the Church teaches us that the Church was born from the side of Jesus, just as Eve was formed from the side of the sleeping Adam. St. John Chrysostom gave this interpretation while teaching the catechumens. Quoting the words, "there came out from his side water and blood," he said,

Dearly beloved, do not pass the secret of this great mystery by without reflection. For I have another secret mystical interpretation to give . . . For as at that time God took a rib from Adam's side and formed woman, so Christ gave us blood and water from his side and formed the Church. Just as then he took the rib while Adam was in a deep sleep, so now he gave the blood and water after his death . . . As a woman feeds her child with her own blood and milk, so too Christ himself continually feeds those whom he has begotten with his own blood (from the Office of Readings, Good Friday).

In the Church all over the world, Christians celebrate the Divine Mercy of the Lord, and the picture used in this devotion shows the Risen Lord Jesus from whose pierced side flow shafts of light in the form and color of blood and water. This devotion is a gift of the Church to us who long for a deeper relationship with Jesus.

O the depth of the riches and wisdom and knowledge of God! How unsearchable are his judgments and how inscrutable his ways!

Our devotions to the Divine Mercy and the Sacred Heart of Jesus are celebrations pointing to the Heart of Jesus full of new life, mercy, love, and compassion for all those who come to him.

In the sacred scriptures, we see that the heart of our God is always open towards all who seek him and come to him in faith. The pierced side of Jesus is a constant reminder of the great love of God the Father. For this love, Jesus lay down his life to the point of shedding every drop of his blood for the salvation of all. Hence, we must guard against making these devotions just sentimental or routine devotions.

Let us come to the heart of Jesus and ask for graces for ourselves and for the whole world. This world is so full of pain and misery because of sin and selfishness. Let us intercede for our country and all the nations to be delivered of oppression, corruption, and terrorism, and ask for God's mercy and the grace of reconciliation, harmony, and understanding between peoples and nations.

Heart of Jesus, burning with love for us, set our hearts on fire with love for thee!

The Prophet Malachi

MALACHI 3:1-2; 4:2; 5-6

Behold, I send my messenger to prepare the way *before me, and the Lord whom you seek will suddenly come to his temple; the* messenger of the covenant *in whom you delight, behold, he is coming, says the* LORD *of hosts. But who can endure the day of his coming, and who can stand when he appears? (Mal 3:1-2, emphasis added).*

In the person of John the Baptist we see the messenger who comes to prepare the way before the Lord. He is the one born of Mother Mary's cousin Elizabeth (cf. Lk 1:57ff). When Mary visited Elizabeth, both Elizabeth and John the Baptist, who was in his mother's womb, were filled with the Holy Spirit (Lk 1:41). When John grew up he went into the wilderness and remained there till the time when God sent him to the people. The prophet Malachi speaks the following words of the Lord about him,

> *Behold, I will send you Elijah the prophet before the great and terrible day of the* LORD *comes. And he will turn the hearts of fathers to their children and the hearts of children to their fathers, lest I come and smite the land with a curse* (Mal 4:5-6).

Jesus testified to the fact that John was the prophet Elijah, sent again by God. After the experience of the transfiguration of Jesus, in which Moses and Elijah also appeared, the disciples asked Jesus about Elijah and when he would come again.

> [Jesus] replied, "Elijah does come, and he is to restore all things; but I tell you that Elijah has already come, and they did not know him, but did to him whatever they pleased. So also the Son of man will suffer at their hands." Then the disciples understood that he was speaking to them about John the Baptist (Mt 17:11-13).

The ministry of John the Baptist was that of reconciliation, as the prophet Malachi had said, "He will turn the hearts of fathers to their children and the hearts of children to their fathers" (Mal 4:6). In the Gospel accounts we see John in the wilderness, and also going into "all the region about the Jordan, preaching a baptism of repentance for the forgiveness of sins ..." (Lk 3:3).

His preaching was so powerful and effective that the people wondered whether he was the Messiah whom they were expecting. But John gave testimony to the coming Messiah saying,

> but he who is mightier than I is coming, the thong of whose sandals I am not worthy to untie; he will baptize you with the Holy Spirit and with fire (Lk 3:16).

John spoke of Jesus the Christ who is the Lord and messenger of the new covenant. He is the one about whom the prophet Malachi spoke saying, "the Lord whom you seek will suddenly come to his temple; the messenger of the covenant in whom you delight, behold, he is coming" (Mal 3:1).

In our earlier reflections on Ps 24 we saw the Lord coming to his temple, and in Jer 31:31f we saw how Jesus is the messenger of the new covenant in his blood. Now let us dwell on the radiant face of Jesus who is the "sun of righteousness." Malachi proclaims the word of the Lord, saying, "But for you who fear my name *the sun of righteousness* shall rise, with healing in its wings" (Mal 4:2, emphasis added).

Jesus said, "I am the light of the world; he who follows me will not walk in darkness, but will have the light of life" (Jn 8:12), and "as long as I am in the world, I am the light of the world" (Jn 9:5).

When the face of Jesus shines upon us we can be sure that all darkness will leave and only radiance and brightness will remain in our lives. Therefore, let us open our lives to his light and allow all the dark areas of our lives of sin and confusion to be taken away by his healing words.

The prophet Isaiah also rejoiced in this marvelous truth as he prophesied saying,

The people who walked in darkness have seen a great light; those who lived in a land of deep darkness, on them has light shined (Is 9:2).

With the light of Jesus comes hope and confidence. All despair and discouragement give way to strength of faith and joy. This is why there is healing in his wings, that is, in the shade of Jesus' love. His light brings comfort, freedom, and rest. His radiance in our hearts enables us to keep his words that bring us life and knowledge of the truth (cf. Jn 6:63b). Let us bask in the light of Jesus, the Sun of righteousness, who rises upon us with healing in his wings. Amen.

CONCLUSION

Thinking about how I got the idea to write this book, the two people who come to mind are Sr. Briege McKenna, O.S.C., and Fr.
Kevin Scallon, C.M. In November 2002, Sr. Briege inspired me with
a word of knowledge and asked me to read the Sacred Bible not just
for teaching others, but for my own spiritual nourishment as well.
In a prophetic vision, she saw me put together a jigsaw puzzle that
gave shape to the radiant face of Jesus as I worked on it from the
center outward.

Acting on that word, I started reading the Bible from cover to
cover again, this time for my own spiritual nourishment, for a
deeper encounter with God, the Father of our Lord Jesus Christ
and our Father. As I read through the Old Testament, my imagination and memory would often take me to the life of Jesus, and I
would stop to relish the face of Jesus every now and then. I could
not keep this treasure to myself, I wanted to share it with everyone, so I felt moved to write this book.

The words of St. Laurence of Brindisi (1559-1619) echo in my
mind, and I would like to share them with you. Preaching about
the word of God, he said:

> The word of God is light to the mind and fire to the will,
> enabling (us) to know and to love God . . . For the soul, it
> is a spiritual treasure-house of merits, and so is called (cf.
> Ps 19:10) gold and very precious stones.

How true! Most of us sincerely want to know and love God, and I am convinced that we can do this better by making the word of God the light for our life and its paths. Therefore, we must rouse ourselves from the heavy slumber of spiritual lethargy and stand up to listen attentively to the words written and proclaimed by the sacred writers in the Bible. For, as the same saint continues,

> To the interior (person) who lives by grace for the Spirit of God, the word is bread and water; it is a bread sweeter than honey from the comb, a water better than milk or wine.

St. Teresa of the Child Jesus also shared similar sentiments. In her *Autobiography* she wrote:

> When I read all those learned books about righteousness and holiness, my poor little brain is quickly fatigued and my heart dried up. Then I put away those learned volumes and I turn to the sacred scriptures — then all becomes light and refreshment.

Desiring that more Catholic Christians discover the riches of the Bible, Vatican II has insisted:

> Such is the force and power of the word of God that it can serve the Church as her support and vigor, and the children of the Church as strength for their faith, food for the soul, and a pure and lasting fount of spiritual life . . . Just as from constant attendance at the Eucharistic mystery the life of the Church draws increase, so a new impulse of spiritual life may be expected from increased veneration of the word of God (*Dei Verbum*, 21, 26).

This is because there is a special power in the word of God not found in any other literature. God's word *effects* what it *proclaims* (cf. Is 55: 10). Therefore, the more the word of God is used by the faithful, the more it will contribute to a vibrant discipleship.

In fact, the Holy Spirit *is* bringing about a tremendous revival of love for the Bible at the grass-roots level of the Church, leading to the formation of thousands of Bible-study groups and numerous publications on the Scriptures. Through these, the Holy Spirit is bringing new strength and vitality to the Body of Christ. Our own Catholic Bible Institute in Mumbai, together with innumerable other members of the worldwide Catholic Biblical Federation (and not forgetting the immense work of our Protestant brothers and sisters), are among these fortunate instruments of the Spirit, working "that the word of the Lord may speed on and triumph" (2 Thess 3:1).

The Bible is a vast treasure, whose spiritual riches still wait to be tapped by many Christians. But for those who are ready to spend time daily in becoming familiar with God's written word, a wonderful experience awaits them, of an abiding inner joy and peace, and the power to live their Christian lives more authentically in today's world. The Bible is also the best *school* of Prayer. Various prayer seminars today may try to teach the theory and techniques of prayer according to various religions and cults, but the reality of prayer lies in *an encounter with the true God*, and it is the Bible, God's written word, that mediates in a very unique and special way God's loving and powerful presence.

Let us, then, come daily to feast on this bread and water of the living word of God, a banquet which the Lord God has prepared for us, as we journey towards our eternal happiness to join him and live with him forever.

Finally, I would like to share with you, dear reader, the words of St. Augustine, as I make them my own:

I have not sought from You some prize that is outside of you, but your face. "Thy face, Lord, do I seek." With perseverance I will insist on this search; I will not seek, in fact, something of little worth, but your face, O Lord, to love you freely, given that I do not find anything more precious... "Turn not thy servant away in anger," so that in seeking you, I come across something else. What can be a greater sorrow than this for the one who loves and seeks the truth of your face? (*Commentaries on the Psalms*, Ps 27:8-9).

ACKNOWLEDGMENTS

I am sincerely grateful to Cardinal Ivan Dias, Archbishop of Bombay, India, for granting me the *Imprimatur* for this book.

Deep gratitude and sincere appreciation for Fr. Fio Mascarenhas, S.J., who edited this work and gave constructive observations and insightful suggestions. Without his support, this work would never have been completed.

Special thanks to Sr. Briege McKenna, O.S.C., and Fr. Kevin Scallon, C.M., whose words inspired me and led me to write this book.

Heartfelt thanks to Mr. Alexander Schweitzer for writing the Foreword of this book even amidst such a hectic and busy schedule in his service of the biblical pastoral ministry worldwide.

Sincere thanks to all my friends, family, and colleagues who have accompanied me in their prayers.

May the Lord Jesus make his radiant face to shine on all those who have encouraged me as I wrote this book.